Margaret Thatcher's Revolution

Margaret Thatcher's Revolution

How it happened and what it meant

Edited by

Subroto Roy

and

John Clarke

continuum
LONDON • NEW YORK

Continuum
The Tower Building, 11 York Road, London SE1 7NX
80 Maiden Lane, Suite 704, New York NY 10038

www.continuumbooks.com

First published 2005

British Library Cataloguing-in-Publication Data
A catalogue record for this book is available from the British Library.

ISBN 0-8264-8484-0

Typeset by Kenneth Burnley, Wirral, Cheshire
Printed and bound in Great Britain by Cromwell Press Ltd, Trowbridge, Wilts

Contents

Contents

Preface

by Sir Peregrine Worsthorne

This excellent book has reminded me why, from the beginning of 'the Thatcherite era' to the bitter end, I was an ardent fan, devoted both to the person and the creed. So far as the person is concerned our first meeting was in the 1960s, in the dining car on a train heading north to Blackpool for the Conservative Party Conference. Mrs Thatcher was then only a fairly small-fry junior minister and I clearly remember my sense of frustration at finding that the only free seat in the dining car was the one next to her, my journalist colleagues and competitors having got in first in seats next to all the news- and gossip-worthy Tory giants like R. A. Butler and Harold Macmillan. Most unpromisingly, to begin with, she resolutely refused to take her head out of her papers and only after at least five minutes of concentrated reading did she give me an opportunity to offer her a drink, which she gladly accepted as was, I soon discovered, her wont. Never over 50 years has my expense account been put to better use. For when much later she suddenly won the leadership, I was marginally less ignorant about her, and closer to her, than most of my colleagues who had been concentrating on the bigger fry.

Was that why I became a Thatcherite? In the first place it probably was. As the only political writer on the *Sunday Telegraph* who knew her, she had become, thanks to that lunch, my property, so to speak, which gave me a personal interest in increasing her value. Ideological affinities came into it as well. In the contest for the leadership following Ted Heath's defeat in the 1974 election, the

Sunday Telegraph invited all the contenders to write articles setting out their stalls, and Margaret Thatcher was the only one even to mention INFLATION, which all the others seemed to accept as a natural and therefore inevitable evil best swept under the carpet. That, so far as I was concerned, was the clincher, and apart from one article by me during her premiership castigating her tone of 'bourgeois triumphalism', the *Sunday Telegraph's* support was unstinted right up to her downfall and after.

Moreover I think I may have even been one of the last people to visit her in Downing Street on the night of her downfall. She was no longer PM. The power lines had suddenly been cut, the red telephones removed and Bernard Ingham, her press secretary, was at his wits' end to find people to help her through those agonizing hours. In the good old days, of course, such visits were relatively brief, with Bernard popping in to say that one's time was up. Not on this occasion. I was the last on the list and she had all the time in the world to spare. Never have the minutes gone more slowly. Everything, past, present and future was too painful to talk about. No sooner did I start opening my mouth than I had to bite my tongue off for fear of opening old wounds and new. For the most part we sat in silence. Eventually, kind and practical to the last, she put an end to the agony by arranging for the occasion to be recorded by a photographer for my scrapbook, even managing to put on the customary smile, which was more than I was able to do. Then saddest twist of all, descending the Downing Street staircase I ran into Carol Thatcher carrying up a large string bag containing, she angrily informed me, 'Mum's dinner', the civil service staff having already been withdrawn.

As to the person, something very sad has happened. Increasingly nowadays, when I think of the blessed Margaret, her face gets mixed up with that of the wicked Dame Shirley Porter, Westminster's gerrymanderess in chief. It is as if the Dame had metamorphosed into Margaret's doppelganger or evil sister. This is deeply unfair, since Margaret loathed Shirley. But somehow or other with the passage of time these two very different characters – the former painstakingly decent and the latter ruthlessly self-serving – have come to seem the two sides of the same coin, rather as in the memory of someone who has undergone a brutal police interrogation, the good cop and the bad cop must just come to seem part of the same nightmare. The lustre of the economic achievements has also faded. While none would be so foolish as to deny them, neither would anybody be so foolish as to go on choosing the word 'miracle' – shades of divine intervention – to describe something which has become so indelibly associated with the powers below rather than the powers above.

This is my only complaint about this book: that it does not take into account the extent of the revulsion that the Thatcherite revolution still arouses: a revulsion so great that the new leader of the Conservative party has felt it necessary to launch a counter-Thatcher revolutionary crusade. Indeed some of the most brilliant and original of the essays contained in the book advocate reigniting the Thatcher revolution. What is more, in terms of logical analysis, their arguments make a lot of sense. The trouble is, however, that any attempt 'to provide a scaffolding for a new and coherent public conversation about the Thatcher revolution' – which this book specifically aims to do – should start with an understanding of the moral damage it did, destroying the very order of high quality people required to implement any major social advance. Not that this was the Thatcherite revolution's intention, any more than it was the French Revolution's to produce Napoleon Bonaparte. But that is the trouble with revolutions, and with wars too, for that matter: they almost always – because their success depends on a willingness, even an eagerness, to exploit ugly passions, crude demagogy and extremist policies – do more harm than good, replacing something bad with something worse.

Which is why, of course, Mrs Thatcher's three previous Conservative prime ministers, Harold Macmillan and Ted Heath – who coined the phrase about the unacceptable fate of capitalism – and Sir Alec Douglas Home leant over backwards to avoid confrontation. This did not spring from Tory wetness, as Mrs Thatcher cheaply alleged, but from a statesmanlike awareness that once the genie of populism is let out of the bottle in a good Conservative cause – to break the power of the leftwing trade unions, for example – there is no knowing to what bad radical cause – destruction of the monarchy and House of Lords, say – it will take up next. Unquestionably Britain's economy was suffering at that time from the postwar consensus about at all cost avoiding mass unemployment and industrial confrontation, but her predecessors, in their wisdom, took the view that not confronting the unions was a necessarily high economic price to pay for hanging on to a constitutional mixture of monarchy, aristocracy and democracy which, in spite of – or perhaps because of – its anachronistic composition, had the best record of any European country in the twentieth century for retaining the consent of the vulgar, while remaining open to the influence of the wise.[1] In other words, it was, on balance, worth sacrificing a lot of market-force economic growth to avoid the risk of parliamentary democracy being superseded by plebiscatory democracy: i.e. mobocracy.

What has to be understood is that ever since universal enfranchisement, the Conservative party's fundamental purpose has been to contain populist pressures from below; pressures arising quite as much from the excesses of the rich as the poor, by comparison with which sorting out the economy – Mrs Thatcher's priority – came a poor second. Something very similar was also true in former times of the parliamentary Labour party, which was just as concerned to water down leftwing doctrinaire socialism in the interest of social peace, as the Tory party was to do the same with doctrinaire capitalism. Both main parties took the view that it was more important to preserve social peace than to promote ideology, and for this purpose it was necessary to hang on to institutions and elites with the weight of history behind them; institutions and elites moreover with a proven record of eliciting civilized and authoritative leadership with a minimum of coercion.

---

1 Vide, Edward Skidelsky, *No More Heroes*, Prospect March 2006.

In short, economic growth was not the top priority. The top priority was to keep intact the English constitution, of which monarchy, aristocracy, democracy – in constantly adjustable proportions – were essential ingredients and if this meant watering down socialism or capitalism, then that was what responsible statesmanship was in duty bound to do.

Mrs Thatcher thought quite differently. To her mind, institutions with the weight of history behind them were the problem, not the solution. They were the problem because the gentlemanly tradition of public service – to justify privilege – they underpinned stood in the way of market forces; diluted the pure capitalist doctrine as advocated by her hero and mentor, Professor Friedrich Hayek. In other words, her faith in capitalism was not only far more absolute than that of her Conservative predecessors', but also more absolute than any previous Labour prime minister's in socialism. (None, in the case of Harold Wilson, who used to boast to his cabinet colleagues of never having read beyond the first paragraph of Karl Marx's *Das Capital*.)

The contrast with Mrs Thatcher could not be greater. For in her Manichean's eye, socialism – in the fold of which she included traditional *noblesse oblige* Tory paternalism – was quite simply evil and capitalism – so long as applied rigorously by true believers – quite simply good. No room in her army for doubters or sceptics; in a word, Conservative wets, whom she blamed for the Conservative party's flirtation with neo-corporatist economic policies, condemned by her as a conspiracy between big business and the large trade unions to do down the self-employed, the skilled workers and small businessman. Here, I believe, we come to the worm in the apple of the Thatcherite revolution: the extent to which it depended not only on the promotion of capitalism but, with even greater passion, on the demotion of everything that, over the centuries, had played a part in producing what the American philosopher, George Santayana once described as England's 'sweet, just boyish masters' – i.e. the least heavy-handed governing class in all history.

I got a whiff of what this might mean soon after Mrs Thatcher came to power when I took an aide of hers – whom she subsequently knighted – out to dinner at The Garrick Club, where he dispelled the customary good cheer by declaring, in rasping tones and eyes ablaze, that not only would he be willing 'to die for the lady but to kill for her as well': an alien kind of language not only unacceptable in the Garrick but, ever since the religious conflicts of the seventeenth century, unacceptable pretty well everywhere else in England as well. Doctrinal extremism was also common parlance among some of the gurus, one of whom I can remember arguing that even individual charity should be discouraged because it interfered with the long-term impersonal wisdom of economic laws.

Nor were these zealotries merely rhetorical or theoretical. For the physical methods later adopted by the Thatcher revolution to put down the Scargill miners were equally alien, owing more to France's brutal revolutionary tradition of treating all protests as incipient insurrections – a tradition loyally upheld by the CRS to this day – than to Britain's preference for seeking agreement over beer and sandwiches in Downing Street. True, Britain's economic plight in the 1970s was bad, very bad, with trade-union thuggery so shameless and provocative as to excuse, if not the proverbial man on the white horse, then at least an indignant iron lady wielding a handbag, quite happy to meet dirty trick with dirty trick. Even so, some of the people she employed to do her dirty work were quite inexcusably awful – right-wing macho ex-public school strike breakers of an order of humanity, or rather of inhumanity, horribly reminiscent of the Black and Tans recruited by Lloyd George to terrorize Ireland after the First World War, the main difference being that whereas Lloyd George's lot of bruised apples modelled themselves on Bulldog Drummond, Mrs Thatcher's lot took their cue from Alan Clark.

Worse, unlike her great Conservative predecessor, Stanley Baldwin, who, after breaking the General Strike in 1926 went on to call for 'peace in our time', Mrs Thatcher seemed to rejoice in the defeat of the miners – her own kith and kin after all – with scarcely more sensitivity than she rejoiced during the Falklands War in the sinking of the Argentinian cruiser, The Belgrano, the prestige accruing from these two victories being exploited to pursue her revolutionary purpose of replacing all forms of class rule – not only aristocratic and proletarian but also bourgeois – in favour of rule by Adam Smith's famous 'hidden hand', the closest human embodiment of which is today's omnipresent accountant, than whom there has never been in all history a top dog figure so totally devoid of charisma.

Why bourgeois, for Heaven's sake? Surely middle-class values are Mrs Thatcher's thing? Very much only up to a point, because in the Victorian age bourgeois high-flyers had deserted commerce and business to form an intellectual aristocracy or Mandarinate serving on merit in high positions throughout the public services and professions, and even, shock, horror, more committed to *noblesse oblige* values than was the hereditary aristocracy itself: in Mrs Thatcher's book, therefore, part of the problem rather than part of the solution. So the Thatcherite version of the revolutionary cry *ecrasez l'infame* applied to pretty much the whole governing class, since taints of the dreaded ambivalence about capitalism could be found among all the elites and all the institutions – legal, military, ecclesiastic, academic and media – notably the BBC – leaving them all wide open to the Thatcherite charge of having committed crimes against the people. There was, however, one entirely innocent exception, the hidden hand of the market which must henceforth reign all the more supreme and unchallenged as a reward and vindication for having been so reduced and ignored during the years of the collective consensus.

In any case the hidden hand was ideologically required as well, being part of the Hayekian doctrine. For anyone who believes, as Mrs Thatcher does absolutely, in the market as self-regulating and morally sufficient is bound to deplore any kind of human intervention as *lese majeste* and although a Marxist-type State intervention – as practised in the Soviet Union – might seem the worst of all on paper, a patrician-mandarin paternalist type intervention, of the English variety, was in practice even more objectionable, having in the past been so guilty of dissolving revolutionary pressures – a sufficient reason, one might have thought, for preserving it at all costs.

In the event, Mrs Thatcher was deposed, with her revolution incomplete. But that did not matter since she left an heir, Tony Blair, only too willing, for different reasons, to carry it on. For in the climate created by the complete collapse of the communist empire, it became more and more difficult for the Labour party to maintain its socialist reservations about capitalism. So the problem was how to come to terms with capitalism without provoking the Left beyond endurance. The solution was pretty obvious. To take the heat off economic inequality, and concentrate radical zeal instead on social and cultural inequality which meant, in effect, joining Mrs Thatcher's revolutionary crusade to de-legitimize and demoralize the very same patrician-mandarinate elites and institutions which were already in her line of fire. So today, for the first time, there is a new political consensus within both the main parties: that the rich and educated are alright so long as they do not give themselves gentlemanly and superior airs, such as assuming that it is the duty of the rich and educated to set an example to the poor and uneducated in matters of taste, manners and morality – a consensus, of course, which the populist tabloid press, as much in the *Daily Mail* as in the *Sun*, is only too happy to endorse and enforce.

So we come back to the fate of all revolutions always to have unintended consequences. The Thatcher revolution, for the very best of reasons, intended to create a Britain fit for practical entrepreneurs to make money, but while triumphantly achieving that goal – indeed because of so triumphantly achieving that goal – it has ended up creating a Britain unsympathetic, not to say positively hostile, to all the other styles and forms of authoritative leadership necessary in a civilized society, including – which we may come to regret – authoritative working-class leadership in the trade unions. As a result we now have, on the one hand, a dynamic economy which provides the public with unprecedented large quantities of public money, but on the other, a society so dismally lacking in leaders endowed with qualities that inspire trust that nothing any longer works in the way it is meant to work. If you doubt me, when next visiting a friend or patient in hospital, try asking for the doctor or nurse in charge. No such person exists. He or she has been replaced by the invisible hand – i.e. an equally invisible money man with eyes only for the bottom line – and you won't get much joy out of him.

Nor is this only true of hospitals, and the public services generally. It is also true, alas, of the professions. There, too, the same money-making priorities are draining away the very quality – that those involved were in it for motives that transcend financial gain – which gave the professions their authoritative status in the first place. A tiny example. For years, family solicitors were able to 'waste' time exchanging personal news with clients before 'getting down to business'. Now this civilized practice has had to be abandoned because the new young partners, very often from top public schools, insist that every minute 'wasted' should be charged for, lest the profit margins suffer. Needless to say, money always came into it at least marginally but not centrally, as is the case today when altruists are made to feel that they are letting the side down. That is the difference. Whereas in the pre-Thatcherite days it was a badge of professional pride to rise above the dictates of market forces, today any professional seeking to do so feels in duty bound to keep quiet about such backward-looking tendencies.

No, let me repeat, I am not just talking about the de-legitimization and demoralization of the old patrician styles of leadership, but of the all the old styles of leadership, ecclesiastical, academic, parliamentary, trade union and even most recently, of the police, as the embarrassingly unimpressive figure of the present Metropolitan Police Commissioner, Sir Ian Blair, makes so unmistakeably clear. Of course fun used to be made of the old officer class, but even George Orwell was the first to thank God in 1940 for its continuing existence. For all his faults Colonel Blimp, like Kipling's Tommy Atkins, was always there when the band begins to play. Not any more, utterly in the case of Colonel Blimp and increasingly – truth to tell – in the case of the Tommy Atkinses who are giving up the Queen's shillings for the richer pickings in the private sector.

Of course these changes are not due only to the Thatcher revolution. Before that there had been all the subversive 'me-first', counter-culture social pressures released during the upheavals of the 1960s and 70s. To that extent the Thatcher revolution was only the economic culmination of a revolutionary era that hollowed out all the old elites and institutions, leaving a vacuum of authority at the top waiting to be filled by nothing more substantial than one lot of middle-class cliques after another. Essentially, the real trouble was one of pace. There can be no doubt that at the time she came to power there was a *practical necessity* to break the power of the trade unions; and another *practical necessity* to liberate market forces. But to the business of attending to these *practical necessities*, she characteristically brought a wholly inappropriate degree of religious passion; a degree of passion appropriate only to the pursuit of a moral ideal. Therein lay the tragedy. The ideal unsurprisingly, never materialized. While dreaming of creating a Britain fit for her father, Alderman Roberts, to live in, Mrs Thatcher has left us a Britain fit only for the likes of her son Mark to live in: not exactly a legacy for which it was worth sacrificing an old order which had successfully kept the British ship of state on an even keel through the excesses of fascism and communism in the twentieth century, and would have been ideally suited to do the same for the excesses of capitalist triumphalism in the twenty-first.

So perhaps all I am saying is that in spite of, or perhaps because of, the excellence of this book, it should come with the following health warning: 'Thatcherism can *unintentionally* seriously damage a body politic's moral health.' With that proviso I can unreservedly recommend it.

Acknowledgements

This volume originated when Subroto Roy returned to Britain after 24 years to become Harold Wincott Visiting Professor of Economics at the University of Buckingham in 2004, and met Dennis O'Keeffe, the editor of *The Salisbury Review*. The volume originated as a special edition of *The Salisbury Review* and thanks are owed to Merrie Cave, Managing Editor, for her encouragement. Dennis O'Keeffe has been *de facto* a third editor of the volume. Thanks are owed to the University of Buckingham for having made Subroto Roy's stay possible, though the University has not been involved in the project and is not responsible for its contents. Thanks are owed to Professor Patrick Minford and Cardiff University for assisting in the production process and to Professor Roger Backhouse, Mr Malcolm Rees and Mrs Linda Waterman for helpful comments.

Notes on Contributors

Norman Tebbit served in the Thatcher Government from 1979–87 as Secretary of State for Employment, and Secretary of State for Trade & Industry. He and his wife were seriously injured in the IRA Brighton bombing in 1984. His early career as a journalist was diverted to civil aviation, following National Service where he trained as a fighter pilot. He was a Member of the House of Commons from 1970–92, when he moved to the House of Lords as Baron Tebbit of Chingford.

Malcolm Rifkind served in the Thatcher and Major Governments from 1979–97. He was Foreign Secretary from 1995–97, Secretary of State for Defence from 1992–95, and a Minister in the Foreign and Commonwealth Office from 1982–86. In 1997 he was knighted for his public services.

George P. Shultz served President Ronald Reagan as the sixtieth Secretary of State of the United States of America from July 1982 to January 1989. He is a recipient of the Medal of Freedom.

Christopher Booker is co-author of *The Great Deception: The Secret History of the European Union* (Continuum 2003); his weekly column in the *Sunday Telegraph* has reported on EU-related issues since 1992. He has just published *The Seven Basic Plots: Why We Tell Stories*, also with Continuum. He was the first editor of *Private Eye*.

Patrick Minford has taught economics at Liverpool University from 1976–97 and at Cardiff Business School, Cardiff University, since then. He was a member of the Monopolies and Mergers Commission 1990–96, and one of HM Treasury's Panel of Forecasters ('6 Wise Men') 1993–96. His work includes *The Supply-Side Revolution in Britain* (Edward Elgar for IEA, 1991). He was awarded a CBE for services to economics in 1996.

Milton Friedman is pre-eminent among modern economists. He has said in the context of this book: 'The "great man" theory of history may not be wholly true, but it is not wholly false. And Margaret Thatcher was a "great man".' His memoirs, with Rose Friedman, *Two Lucky People*, were published by the University of Chicago Press in 1998.

Martin Ricketts teaches economics at the University of Buckingham. His interests have been in the economics of public finance, public choice, privatization, regulation and housing. His work includes *The Economics of Business Enterprise* (Edward Elgar, 3rd edn, 2002) and, with Michael G. Webb, *The Economics of Energy* (Macmillan 1980). In 1991–92, he was Economic Director of the National Economic Development Office, and is an Honorary Professor at the Edinburgh Business School.

Patricia Morgan is author or co-author of *Delinquent Fantasies* (Temple Smith 1978), *Families in Dreamland* (Social Affairs Unit 1992), *Farewell to the Family?* (IEA, 2nd edn, 1999), *Are Families Affordable?* (Centre for Policy Studies 1996), *Who Needs Parents?* (IEA 1996), *Adoption and the Care of Children* (IEA 1998), *Adoption: The Continuing Debate* (IEA 1999), *Marriage-Lite* (Institute for the Study of Civil Society 2000) and *Children as Trophies* (Christian Institute 2002). She has contributed to numerous other periodicals, newspapers and books including *Juvenile Delinquency in the United States and the United Kingdom* (Macmillan 1999).

Dennis O'Keeffe has taught pupils and teachers for over forty years, and at present teaches social science at the University of Buckingham. His most recent book is a translation of Constant's *Principles of Politics*. His other works include *The Wayward Elite* (Adam Smith Institute 1991), and *Truancy in English Secondary Schools* (HMSO 1993).

James Tooley's publications include *The Global Education Industry: Lessons from Developing Countries* (IEA 2001), and *Reclaiming Education* (Cassell 2001). He co-edited with **James Stanfield** *Government Failure: E. G. West on Education* (IEA 2003). They are part of a team at the E. G. West Centre, School of Education, University of Newcastle upon Tyne, whose current research seeks to draw lessons from the growth of private schools for low income families in developing countries.

James Stanfield is a member of the team at the E. G. West Centre, School of Education, University of Newcastle upon Tyne.

Terence Kealey's biomedical research at Oxford and Cambridge focused on the cell biology of human skin. His work includes *The Economic Laws of Scientific Research* (Macmillan 1996) and *Sex, Science and Profits* (Macmillan 2005).

David Marsland taught for many years at Brunel University. His academic interests have been in healthcare, education and the penal system. His works include *Seeds of Bankruptcy* (Claridge Press 1988), and *Welfare or Welfare State?* (Macmillan 1996). In 1991 he was the first recipient of the Thatcher Award for analysis of freedom.

Norman Barry teaches politics at the University of Buckingham. His work includes *Hayek's Social and Economic Philosophy* (Macmillan 1979), *On Classical Liberalism and Libertarianism* (Macmillan 1986), *The New Right* (Croom Helm 1987), *Welfare*

(Open University Press 1999), *Business Ethics* (Macmillan 1998), and *An Introduction to Modern Political Theory* (Macmillan, 4th edn, 2000).

William Hague has served as the Member of Parliament for Richmond, Yorkshire, since 1989, and was the Leader of the Opposition in Parliament from 1997 until June 2001. He has recently published a political biography, *William Pitt the Younger* (HarperCollins 2004).

John Clarke teaches history at the University of Buckingham with a special interest in international politics. His works include **George III** (Weidenfeld 1972), *England in the Age of Cobbett* (Allen and Unwin 1977), and *British Diplomacy and Foreign Policy* (Routledge 1989).

Subroto Roy's *Philosophy of Economics* (Routledge 1989) applied John Wisdom and Renford Bambrough to solving extant problems in economic theory. During the Thatcher Era, *The Times* wrote its lead editorial of 29 May 1984 about his critique of Indian economic policy. He led 'perestroika' projects for India and Pakistan at the University of Hawaii in the late 1980s, and contributed to the origins of India's 1991 economic reform as a senior adviser to Rajiv Gandhi in the months preceding the latter's assassination. He is a citizen of the Indian Republic.

Editorial Introduction

Few periods in British history can have been as dispiriting as the 1970s. Phrases of the times, such as 'the British disease', 'stag-flation', 'the winter of our discontent', 'the three day week', etc., evoke painful memories. The spell of communism continued to enthral many among Britain's academic and intellectual elite. The great Victorians had been dismissed as hypocrites, the Industrial Revolution seen in terms of suffering endured in the 'Dark Satanic Mills'. Britain's imperial story was supposed to be one merely of racism and incompetence, while it had become difficult to even mention the word 'liberty' at the Ancient Universities. Anglo-American cooperation, so strong and obvious in the Second World War, had eroded. While some looked to the new EEC, hoping the German economic miracle would somehow rub off at home, almost no-one appeared to be seeking solutions from within Britain's own traditions, values and capacities.

This volume puts forward the simple premise that during the Margaret Thatcher premiership Britain came to be greatly trans-formed, mostly for the better, and mostly by Britain pulling herself up by her own bootstraps. We suggest that a distinct 'Thatcher Era' will be identified by future historians as clearly as present-day historians see something like the Battle of Britain – not just as any old humdrum battle but as a decisive turning-point.

It is astonishing that the central facts of the transformation have thus far failed to find their rightful place in Britain's public memory.[1] On the contrary, whether by accident or default or

1

design, the origins of the political and economic transformation have become obscured or even erased. Others who may have had nothing to do with the transformation, or even sought to frustrate it, have come to claim or been attributed credit for it – something that may be as common with creative advances in political economy as it is in technology, science or the arts. This would help explain why British school textbooks and curricula have not until now recorded any 'Thatcher Era'.

For example, a 'major research project' on the UK economy by the most venerable institutions of American and British academic economics, finds itself able in 2004 to praise Margaret Thatcher's 1979 Government – but only with faint damns.[2] An 'unhappy electorate' is said to have voted her Government into office despite its 'most doctrinaire' nature. Ideas 'came in part from the growing influence of *laissez-faire* critics' and a footnote says '[t]he arguments of Friedrich Hayek and Milton Friedman were widely disseminated'.[3] Keith Joseph is identified as the 'key individual funnelling *laissez-faire* ideas from the right wing into the Conservative Party', and he 'had the ear of the party's leader, Margaret Thatcher'. Yet Thatcher's Revolution is to be seen merely as part of '*the continuing effort of UK governments, from the Conservatives in the 1980s through Labour in the 1990s, to improve economic efficiency in the country by developing more market-friendly policies and economic institutions*'.[4] Norman Tebbit's remark is mentioned that 'his father had not sat around on his backside in the Great Depression moaning about the lack of jobs: he had gotten on his bike and looked for work'. But we are told Tebbit '*is not the only person to have had similar thoughts*'.[5] '[N]umerous government, union, business, and academic experts and leaders in the United Kingdom, *many of whom were involved with developing and introducing these policies*'[6] are said to have been consulted in the project and over 300 names are listed in the Author Index – however, these names do not include Milton Friedman, Alan Walters or Peter Bauer, let alone Ralph Harris, Arthur Seldon, Alfred Sherman, Keith Joseph or others at the Institute of Economic Affairs or Centre for Policy Studies.[7]

We are told '[n]early all groups and political parties' have today 'come to accept many of the initially controversial changes that constituted the "Thatcher Revolution", *albeit with different emphases and concerns over how best to assure that the market reforms benefited society as a whole*'.[8] And 'Britain's economic reforms have been motivated by a desire to increase the reliance on market forces relative to the role of the state in the determination of prices and the allocation of resources . . . the main goal of the UK policy reforms has been to reduce the economic role of the state and enhance the role of markets in determining economic outcomes.' Even if Margaret Thatcher just happened to have started the process, John Major 'pursued a similar agenda' while in 'the late 1990s, Blair's New Labour government continued to introduce market-enhancing reforms'; indeed Mr Blair's speech to the 'World Economic Forum' on 18 January 2000 is quoted as to how he has come to invent 'a Third Way'. In soundbites: '*Supporting wealth creation. Tackling vested interests. Using market mechanisms.*'[9] According to this view, Margaret Thatcher and her friends are to be at best praised with faint damns; certainly no 'Thatcher Era' deserves to be marked in British history.

The present volume provides precise answers to this kind of denial of history that is being attempted in the political economy of contemporary Britain. The chapters that follow establish beyond doubt that a Thatcher Era *is* an identifiable historical phenomenon which altered British political and economic reality permanently, and largely for the better.[10] We seek to be neither hagiographic nor polemical; rather our aim is to get a precise grip on the most important specific facts, clearing away the clutter and exploding myths about how what happened came to happen. In so doing, we hope to provide a scaffolding for a new and coherent public conversation on these subjects in Britain and elsewhere. Those who cannot remember the past are condemned to repeat its mistakes; or, in the words of J. M. Keynes, we need to 'study the present in the light of the past for the purposes of the future'. A muddled understanding of earlier times leads to a muddled understanding of the present, and hence to a muddled sense of the future. Besides, the relevant 'intellectual property rights' involved in this particular advance in political economy ought perhaps to be restored to their original owners.

Norman Tebbit and Malcolm Rifkind were themselves members of Margaret Thatcher's Governments. Tebbit's unique and intimate account of the ideological, organizational and social revolution that occurred among the Tories under Thatcher's leadership is likely to become compulsory reading for every serious student of contemporary British political science.[11] Rifkind's elegant survey of diplomatic and military history demonstrates how victory in the difficult war provoked by Argentina gave Thatcher the courage and authority to tackle larger adversaries like Soviet communism. He points to Thatcher's vital role in persuading Ronald Reagan that the West could engage with Gorbachev's new Russia. Reagan, who became a national leader later than Thatcher, looked to her as an admired friend and counsellor – a view confirmed in the tribute by George P. Shultz which we are privileged to publish.[12]

A crucial aspect of Britain's role in the world concerns the evolution of the common market with her neighbours. Christopher Booker's masterly survey describes the bargaining, negotiation, manoeuvring and brinkmanship that has occurred over thirty years. Thatcher's view of the 'European project' matured as she encountered the realities of what it stood for, in contrast to the partial picture given to the public when Britain joined the Common Market in 1973. Meanwhile the Labour Party moved from outright hostility to 'Europe' towards closer 'harmonization'. A critical point occurred in September 1988 when Jacques Delors 'won an ovation from Britain's trade union leaders in Bournemouth by a speech which contradicted the very basis of Thatcherism'; only days later, Thatcher's Bruges speech trenchantly set out her opposition to an 'artificial mega-state'.[13] Thatcher's concerns isolated her from her closest colleagues and marked the end of the era that had begun with her becoming Tory Leader.

Our next two chapters address economics. Patrick Minford describes how the Thatcher Governments dealt with the high inflation of the 1970s, the structural problems of the fiscal deficit and distortions of the labour market.[14] Minford suggests the European rejection of 'Anglo-Saxon' policies of market liberalization and adoption of the euro have contributed to relative stagnation and a lack of convergence within the euro-zone compared to a vibrant British economy. The Blair Government's economic achievements have been to *not* join the euro and to have *not* reversed Thatcherian macroeconomic policies – indeed to have added to them by making the Bank of England independent, a long-standing proposal of classical liberal economics.[15] We are privileged to add a comment on Minford's chapter by Milton Friedman.

Martin Ricketts describes how the structure of incentives changed in Britain, leading to more efficient use of real resources. Nationalized industries and utilities and the municipal housing stock were 'privatized', restrictions on commerce removed and competition encouraged, notably by ending foreign exchange controls and by the 'big-bang' which deregulated London's financial markets. Organized labour's coercive powers were reduced. Tax reforms reduced top marginal rates and the upward trend of total tax revenue as a proportion of GDP was halted. The scope for the 'politicization' of business decision-making was reduced while that of free competitive market processes widened.

Overall, Margaret Thatcher's premiership ended the chaos of stagnation, unemployment and inflation in Britain, while the structure of individual incentives and market institutions came to be transformed towards greater competitiveness, productivity and technological progress, ushering in a long period of prosperity. The UK's overall rank among 22 OECD countries of 'Economic Freedom' apparently changed as follows:[16]

1970	1975	1980	1985	1990	1995	1999
19	13	15	5	2	2	2

– while a 1999 OECD study placed the UK at 1 out of 21 with respect to the suitability of its regulatory climate for business, e.g. with respect to state control and barriers to entrepreneurship, trade and investment.[17]

Yet Britain's growth of national wealth and technological progress appears to have been accompanied by signs of social collapse in some areas. The early stages of the Industrial Revolution witnessed social fragmentation but the new middle classes, together with a sobered aristocracy, had sensed that rising prosperity must be accompanied by strengthened social institutions. An age which did not have electricity produced great reforms in Parliament, the churches, the monarchy, the armed forces, the civil services, the Ancient Universities, the great Schools with their new sports – all contributed to a living social fabric which helped to absorb the shocks of an alienating marketplace. Has any equivalent phenomenon taken place after the Thatcher Era? If not, why has contemporary British society with its high technology not been able to generate institutional responses appropriate to drastic economic change and rising prosperity?

Some of the institutions that might have been expected to perform this role have themselves been in disarray. The decline of parliamentary politics has been deplored around the world, with political decisions in the age of television being made in lobbies and expensive restaurants, later to be announced at media events, rather than emerging as a result of authentic debate on the floor. Tebbit suggests the Mother of Parliaments has not been immune: '[It] had become a salaried professional business seeking the status of offices, office hours and staff. In the immortal words of Julian Amery, members interpreted their role as representing Parliament in their constituencies rather than their constituencies in Parliament.' Massive majorities of any party, with an opposition collapsing or being eclipsed in the age of television, may have helped to weaken the sense of parliamentary history and traditions. Momentarily, the Church seemed to become the opposition in British politics, but modern churches and religious institutions have their own problems and may have yielded too readily to passing social fashions and hence been in no position to provide the spiritual succour that remains in genuine demand. In particular, the politicized destruction of traditions has created a new order seemingly more egalitarian or homogeneous than what it replaced, but people are left bereft of their past, alternately enervated by the present and fearful and anxious about their future. The lack of a proper response from social institutions to rapid change may have caused old virtues like patience, modesty, fidelity and moderation to give way to old vices like intemperance, promiscuity and untrammelled hedonism, to a coarsening rather than a cultivation or advancement of social tastes, manners, language and culture. 'An age of unreason that is nevertheless not an age of faith.'[18] Is it possible a *surfeit* of individual choices can arise in society, greater than what many children, women and men privately wish for? How does any society find the right balance on questions of autonomy, modesty and protection of family life and other social relationships?

Patricia Morgan, Dennis O'Keeffe, James Tooley and James Stanfield, Terence Kealey and David Marsland probe these kinds of controversial matters in chapters on the family, school education, higher education and research and healthcare in contemporary Britain in the aftermath of the Thatcher Era. Morgan identifies the errors of the Thatcher and Major Governments with respect to the family, exploding the myth that they tried to reimpose a traditional patriarchal model upon a reluctant society; indeed the Tories failed to understand the politically correct 'postmodern' 'counter-culture', and inadvertently made things worse with their laxity in such areas as the divorce and tax laws. If she had a magic wand, Morgan would wave it to remove all laws that, by accident or design, have encouraged the dissolution of the family as normally understood. O'Keeffe points to the manipulation of education by a collectivist-minded elite in the education bureaucracy, resulting in a situation in which millions of children can leave school effectively illiterate and innumerate. Solutions are offered by Tooley and Stanfield, who report on exciting new research applying international models of private education to improve the dismal situation in Britain. (Tooley and Stanfield reproduce with permission as an Appendix to their chapter, an episode from *Yes Prime Minister* on the subject.) Kealey suggests there is no reason for government backing of science and technology, and that the decline of British universities can be arrested only by a mixed system on the American pattern with a vigorous sector of private higher education. Marsland makes the case for 'denationalization' as the only reliable route to reforming British healthcare.

Instead of producing the shibboleths and soundbites that are the common currency of the age of television, these authors have boldly chalked out radical new alternatives. Finally, Norman Barry employs a single hypothesis to explain the Thatcher Revolution from a 'determinist' academic viewpoint, and William Hague reflects on Thatcher's long-term legacy. Hague is certain it will be seen as a decisive turning-point in modern British history, and that Margaret Thatcher herself will long inspire those who believe in economic freedom and political order around the world.

It should not be assumed the editors or individual authors are in any necessary agreement with one another on matters of substance, interpretation or judgement. Indeed there has been methodological pluralism amongst them, ranging across the concrete practicality of Tebbit, Rifkind, and Booker, the analytics of Minford and Ricketts, the stream-of-consciousness descriptions of Morgan, the bold radicalism of O'Keeffe, Tooley and Stanfield, Kealey, and Marsland, the determinism of Barry and the speculation of Hague. Each chapter is an original contribution written for the purposes of this volume, and able to stand independently of the others.[19] The principal responsibility for the substance and accuracy of each chapter rests with its individual author. The responsibility for the choice of subjects and choice of authors, the extent of substantive and stylistic quality control, and the interpretations and judgements contained in this Introduction rest with the editors. Altogether, it is hoped the volume will provide a basis for a new coherent and well-informed public discussion on many issues of importance to Britain's future, and by analogy elsewhere in the world.[20]

Notes

1   We may have expected by now to see widespread and unassailable public recognition of these years having been a vital period of modern British history. A stream of sober evaluations of that achievement may have been expected, with a spill-over recordng this in British school textbooks and curricula. This has not happened and the question arises why not. An enormous literature about Margaret Thatcher herself has of course arisen, and the Thatcher Foundation's website currently observes a gulf in British politics between her 'Critics' and 'Defenders'. Indeed visceral reactions and an emphasis on personality may have impeded understanding of the nature of the transformation that occurred. A few attempts were made to gain a fuller picture during the Thatcher premiership, most notably the 1989 volume *The Thatcher Effect: A Decade of Change* edited by Dennis Kavanagh and Anthony Seldon (Oxford: Clarendon Press). But these could not provide a historical perspective nor have identified the existence of a 'Thatcher Era'. Once Margaret Thatcher departed from power, even such attempts seemed to come to an end.

2   The philosopher Renford Bambrough spoke of 'Praising with Faint Damns' while discussing certain modern theological debates, *Religion and Humanism* (BBC, 1965).

3   Professor John Pencavel of Stanford University, in *Seeking a Premier Economy, The Economic Effects of British Economic Reforms, 1980–2000*, p. 196, edited by David Card, Richard Blundell and Richard B. Freeman (Chicago and London: University of Chicago Press, 2004), the result of a project 'organized jointly by the National Bureau of Economic Research and the Centre for Economic Performance of the London School of Economics and the Economic and Social Research Council for the Microeconomic Analysis of Public Policy at the Institute for Fiscal Studies'.

4   Ibid. p. ix, italics added.

5 Professors Paul Gregg, Stephen Machin and Alan Manning of Bristol University, University College London and the London School of Economics respectively, ibid. p. 378, italics added.

6 Ibid. p. ix, italics added.

7 *Cf. infra* note 11 regarding the specific impact of Joseph and Sherman.

8 Professors David Card, Richard Blundell, Richard B. Freedman of University College London, Princeton University and Harvard University respectively, ibid., pp. 1–2, italics added.

9 Ibid., p. 11, italics added. Thus Mr Blair has felt himself free to castigate as 'typical Tory policy' whatever he wishes, e.g. Prime Minister's Questions on 8 September 2004 at 12.11 pm; at 11.50 am, BBC 2's 'Daily Politics' programme that fed into Prime Minister's Questions that day, showed a member of the public saying to the cameras 'Hi Tony, the Tories are vicious and you're not'.

10 We mean this as a historical hypothesis which would be unaffected by, e.g. Lady Thatcher herself visiting Mr Blair during his premiership.

11 An analysis of the specifically economic dimension stemming from the influence of Keith Joseph and Alfred Sherman may be found in Morrison Halcrow, *Keith Joseph, A Single Mind* (Macmillan 1989).

12 Rifkind observes 'Thatcher, despite her closeness to Reagan, never faced the accusation of being the President's "poodle"'. Indeed Britain's long, well-recorded and broadly positive role in the political history of the world has left her with an abundant store of goodwill and affection. Many nations, the most powerful included, may implicitly look to Britain to set standards and lead by example; thus world-events tend to lose coherence when Britain herself becomes confused or loses her bearings.

13 In the theory of games, a 'saddlepoint' is an example of where the minimal point of one curve is also a maximal point of another curve, as in the seat of a saddle; these two speeches may have marked such a 'saddlepoint'.

14 Minford argues it was the modern quantity theory of money rather than 'incomes policy' that was used in the defeat of inflation by affecting fiscal expectations. After some confusion, the 1981 budget revealed a determination to curb the fiscal deficit. Both inflation and interest rates fell, marking a turning-point in the Thatcher Government's credibility and popularity. Unemployment then became the main issue, Thatcherians taking time to discover the significance of the unemployment benefit regime; once that was done in 1986 unemployment began to fall too. Minford argues there were alternative paths to macroeconomic adjustment depending on which version of the quantity theory was being used. In one version, excessive monetary growth (exceeding growth of real income) was to be slowed down; in doing this and moving to the 'natural rate of unemployment' ('ground out' of the system of Walrasian general equilibrium equations as Milton Friedman put it in his Presidential address to the American Economic Association, 'The Role of Monetary Policy', *American Economic*

Review, 1968), there would be difficult temporary adjustment. (For modern criticism from the point of view of general equilibrium theory and Keynes's economics, see Frank Hahn, *Equilibrium and Macroeconomics* (Boston: MIT Press, 1984) and *Money, Growth and Stability* (Boston: MIT Press, 1985). A dialogue between a Friedmanian and a Hahnian may be found in Subroto Roy, *Philosophy of Economics: On the Scope of Reason in Economic Inquiry* (London and New York: Routledge, 1989).) Minford argues that the British school of rational expectations pointed to excessive monetary growth being caused by an out-of-control fiscal process. Hence the root problem was to tackle the fiscal process, reduce its monetization, and directly affect inflationary expectations and hence inflation.

15 See *In Search of a Monetary Constitution*, edited by Leland C. Yeager (Harvard University Press, 1962).

16 Fraser Institute, *Economic freedom of the world: 2001 annual report*, quoted in Card, Blundell and Freedman (eds) *Seeking a Premier Economy, op.cit.* p. 15. *et. seq*. In specific categories:

Structure of Economy and Use of Markets		Legal Structure and Property Rights		Freedom in Capital/Financial Markets	
1980	1999	1980	1999	1980	1999
11	5	14	3	7	1

17 Giuseppe Nicoletti, Stefano Scarpetta and Oliver Boylaud, 'Summary indicators of product market regulation with an extension to employment practice legislation', OECD, Paris, Working Paper No. 226, 1999.

18 Renford Bambrough, Editorial regarding the Gifford Lectures, *Philosophy*, 1973.

19 Tooley and Stanfield were initially asked for a Comment by us, including reporting on their current research some of which has seen publication before.

20 The problems of political economy in any country are complex and various, and approaches have to be made from and to all schools of thought with open and undogmatic minds in a democratic spirit. As was once said of another ancient democracy: 'Here each individual is interested not only in his own affairs but in the affairs of the state as well; even those who are mostly occupied with their own business are extremely well-informed on general politics – this is a peculiarity of ours: we do not say that a man who takes no interest in politics is a man who minds his own business; we say that he has no business here at all.' Pericles' Funeral Oration, *History of the Peloponnesian War* by Thucydides, II.40, translated by Rex Warner, Penguin 1954.

1 On the inner culture of the Tories

Norman Tebbit

Any appraisal of the impact of Margaret Thatcher upon the culture of the Tory Party requires some definition and explanation of the Party's condition and culture at the time of her accession to the leadership.

Political parties are complex organisms, and the Conservatives have not been an exception. There was a hierarchy with the 'Leader' at its head.[1] Margaret Thatcher was only the second leader to have been elected rather than to have 'emerged', although the electorate in 1975 was still restricted to the Parliamentary Party. The Leader once in office is then supported (whilst he or she holds its confidence) by the Shadow Cabinet or, if in Government, by the Cabinet. They are to the Leader what noblemen were to a Saxon king – with the Parliamentary Party playing the role of housecarls, with militias and irregulars forming the remainder of the army. The second pillar comprises 'Central Office' (one of the militia) seen by Margaret Thatcher as 'constitutionally, the Leader of the Party's Office' (a definition which might not be fully shared by all Party Chairmen). In Opposition, Central Office certainly functions not only as the focal point of the voluntary party, the membership in the country, and as an election machine, but also as a resource for the Leader and the Shadow Cabinet. Whether in Government or Opposition, its importance and activity are closely related to the electoral cycle throughout which it waxes and wanes in significance. All these institutions and activities are supported by the mass membership, their subscriptions and fund-raising and by donations. Until the late 1980s and 1990s, the Conservative Party benefited from substantial funding from major public companies although with changes in both law and practice these have now largely dried up, and 'Short Money' has become increasingly important in sustaining the role of the Opposition and thereby, the Leader's office.

Vastly outnumbering these cadres which constitute the Party, but both influencing and being influenced by it to an extent which almost makes them part of it, are the long-term committed Tory voters. During the inter-War years, a number of Conservative radicals had sought to move the party towards the corporatist policies then popular across Europe. Even during the Second World War, the Tory Reform Committee was active in the House of Commons as a virtual party within a party pressing a paternalist corporatist agenda often in sympathy with Labour's statist policies. After the 1945 election defeat, Winston Churchill created the Conservative Research Department of Central Office; he put R. A. Butler in charge of a 'rethink' of domestic policy which took the party firmly to the left. The key policy document, 'The Industrial Charter' of 1947, largely bought into Harold Macmillan's pre-War corporatist 'Middle Way' (the middle being half way between Manchester and Moscow, or free market liberalism and state communism) supporting the nationalization of the Bank of England, coal and railways, the establishment of state planning and central economic direction, alongside industrial 'co-partnership' and industrial councils.

Experience of the Labour Government of 1945–51, however, led Churchill's administration to bravely begin a 'bonfire of controls', ending rationing, including amidst great controversy rationing of sweets and chocolates, and quietly forgetting about co-partnership. Under Macmillan, the rot set in, and the doctrine of the 'left only ratchet' and the inevitability of the decline of capitalism prevailed. The industrial problems of low labour productivity and excessive union power were answered not with labour law reform but with Keynesian spending and the import of cheap unskilled labour.

The electorate correctly divined that even if they had 'never had it so good', the Conservative Government had lost the plot and in 1964 the voters marginally preferred Labour – a choice confirmed in 1966. By 1970, Labour lost, first its nerve and then the election. The Conservative Party had regrouped under Ted Heath's superficially meritocratic, grammar school, management-consultant style. There was, however, a built-in conflict between Heath's 'right wing' Selsdon agenda[2] and his predominantly centrist or leftist Cabinet, most notably Robert Carr, Peter Walker and Ian Gilmour. Before long, Heath faced powerful and militant union leaders. His legalistic attempts to control union power ended in humiliating failure and the Selsdon agenda was jettisoned in an abject retreat towards the politics of consensus. But the union leaders saw no need for consensus when victory was in their grasp. The Treasury fire-hosed money at the economy whilst seeking to control wages and prices by law, hoping growth might replace inflation. Then, with no adequate response to the coalminers strike, Mr Heath appealed to the electorate. After a hesitant verdict in February 1974 from the voters who wanted him out but were not sure they wanted Harold Wilson in, the country plumped more surely for Labour eight months later in the October election.

Through the 1950s and 1960s much had been made of the great consensus in politics. The extent of the public sector was broadly accepted by all the parties. Steel was in the margin, being nationalized, denationalized and re-nationalized, but otherwise state ownership of industry was almost unchallenged by the Conservative Party. The legal privileges of the trades unions were not even questioned, and the privately owned sector of residential letting was systematically eroded by rent control and tenant protection. More helpfully, NATO membership, nuclear deterrence and the Atlantic Alliance were also common ground of the consensus. In short, it was possible to tell Tweedledum from Tweedledee, but more by packaging and accents than by actions.

Margaret Thatcher is often credited with breaking the post-War political consensus, but it had already begun to fracture by the early 1970s. Heath's attempts to curb union power and impose wage controls by law, together with Wilson's nationalization of shipbuilding and aerospace construction, had led to sharpening of political differences between the major parties. At the same time Labour's Euro-fanatics (who were generally social democrats) were becoming more restive.

Ted Heath's February 1974 election defeat and his vain attempt to entice the Liberals into a coalition which was conducted without consulting the Tory Parliamentary Party, brewed up into a leadership crisis, which boiled over in the wake of the October 1974 defeat. Entirely unexpectedly, Margaret Thatcher emerged as the front runner in the leadership election of 1975 and then the decisive winner.

At that time, the culture of the Party was, like the national electorate at large, muddled and confused. The grassroots membership and the Central Office secretariat were amazed at the action of the Parliamentary Party in electing a woman leader. The Parliamentary Party seemed no less surprised at what it had done, whilst Heath's Shadow Cabinet colleagues were mostly simply outraged.

The typical local Conservative committee members and activists, the lickers of envelopes, deliverers of leaflets, organizers of fêtes, lunches, coffee mornings and dinners, believed still in those days Conservatism to be the natural state of affairs. 'We are not political here – we are Conservatives' was the apocryphal reply of the lower middle class voter being canvassed for support in elections. The typical Conservative election worker took a not dissimilar view and had never accepted the idea that socialism was a historical inevitability, preferring to regard Conservatism as the natural order of things.

Conservatism implied support for the established way of doing things, a commitment to the Crown, the armed forces, police, judiciary, professions, private enterprise and respect for the Church of England whatever one's religious beliefs. The Parliamentary Party was still dominated by public school educated men of an age to have fought in the War, and the 'knights from the shires' were a powerful stabilizing influence. Representative of these was Sir Harry Legge-Bourke, chairman of the 1922 Committee (who retired in 1979). Born in 1914, educated at Eton and Sandhurst, a great traditionalist but with a lively open mind, a man of unimpeachable integrity, he was in Parliament out of a sense of public duty rather than personal ambition.

In her memoirs (Volume 1 *The Path to Power*, p. 290), Margaret Thatcher writes of her difficulty as the newly elected Leader in choosing a Shadow Cabinet which would not be in the shadow of the former regime. 'In fact given the fragility as yet of my position and the need to express a balance of opinion in the Shadow Cabinet to bring the Party together, it was a relatively successful operation.' She faced similar problems at Central Office where 'events during the leadership campaign had convinced me that it would be very difficult for some of those there to act in that capacity under me' (p. 291).

She was no stranger to such a predicament. At the contest for the nomination as candidate for Finchley in 1958, she had defeated the runner-up by the narrowest of margins and the Executive Committee was then unable to achieve the traditional unanimous vote to select her. A hard core could not accept a woman with young children – and a right-wing woman too – as a Conservative Member of Parliament. At the time she became Leader, I described her election as a 'corporals' coup' and certainly neither she, the political ideas for which she stood, nor her social standing, brought her the support of the colonels usually associated with political coups.

Two of her early decisions as Leader were the appointment of her Deputy and the Chairman of the Party. At Central Office she appointed Peter Thorneycroft and as her Deputy, Willie Whitelaw, both Heath loyalists. She chose well for each one was even more a loyalist than a Heathite. Not only were they loyal to her, but both were effective and commanded the support of many others who might otherwise have been reluctant to accept her leadership. They played key roles in cementing her position and facilitating the cultural changes of the Party.

The weakness of Thatcher's position in her early days as Leader sprang only partly from her being a woman, but it was a significant factor. Conservatives, no less than the population at large, were hesitant to believe a woman could resolve the political issues which had defeated notable men. There never had been a woman premier, therefore women did not become Prime Ministers. It was a man's job. After all, what if it came to war? Men fought wars whilst women wept at home. Fortunately for her, in a modern world (and amongst an electorate in which the women have more votes than the men) her opponents did not dare to argue that case.

More dangerous to her was the overwhelming assumption amongst the senior ranks of the Parliamentary Party that Britain could be governed only with the consent, if not the actual approval of the trades unions – which they took to be the, mostly unrepresentative, leaders of those unions. That was at the heart of the post-War consensus. They also believed that inflation was caused by a spiral of price rises sparking huge wage demands and settlements bringing further price rises, and that the spiral could be broken only by a prices and incomes policy. In the minds of that wing of the Party the only question was whether the policy should be statutory or voluntary, but in either case a 'wage rise norm' would be established to which unions and employers would be either cajoled and pressurized or required by law to adhere.

Even after a year of Thatcher's leadership the key policy statement *The Right Approach – a Statement of Conservative Aims* (October 1976) asked the question if there was any alternative to statutory policies or social contracts and gave the answer 'Other countries have found ways'. It gave as its favoured example, 'The West Germans, for example, without any elaborate machinery establish each year a generally agreed basis for responsible wage bargaining. They do, however, make extensive use of consultative procedures – known as Concerted Action – for establishing this basis. However difficult it may be we need to develop a comparable approach that would be compatible with existing British institutions.'

However, while the Tories had been in Opposition from 1974 to 1979, Harold Wilson and then James Callaghan had been driven deeper and deeper into crisis, not only because of their own previous economic policies (notably on tax and spending) but because of the reckless pursuit of extra-Parliamentary political power by the leaders of the trades union movement. Wilson's famous demand (or perhaps a plea) to AUEW leader, Hugh Scanlon: 'Get your tanks off my lawn Hughie' was made in 1969, but throughout the Labour administration of 1974–79, not to mention the Heath years of 1970–74, the tanks were scarcely ever absent from the Prime Ministerial lawn. Labour's difficulties, following those of Ted Heath, raised the union issue, and it was the unbridled arrogance and destructive power of the union movement which finally drove the Callaghan Government to defeat in 1979 in the wake of the Winter of Discontent. It was this which began to give Margaret Thatcher enough wriggle to disassociate herself from the 'Tory Wets'.

Public opinion, and more especially grassroots Tory opinion and that of the Parliamentary Party outside the Shadow Cabinet, was characterized by a mixture of anger and fear. Something, they all agreed, would have to be done about the unions – but what? Appeasement had failed, but so too had Heath's trades union legislation, and before long the question being asked was 'Is Britain becoming ungovernable?'

At the 1979 election a frequent doorstep question was 'But what if the trades union leaders will not talk to Mrs Thatcher?' My reply that 'Mrs Thatcher would be happy as they have nothing sensible to say' was regarded as beyond frivolity and bordering on lunacy.

The question, however, was asked abroad and at home, within and without the Conservative Party, out of longing for a leader strong enough to solve the trades union question – but with a fear that Mrs Thatcher was unlikely to find the answer which had eluded her three predecessors. Jim Prior, her shadow Secretary of State for Employment, spoke for the consensus wing, assuring everyone that since everyone was sensible and full of goodwill, with mutual understanding an agreed answer would manifest itself.

It was fortunate for Mrs Thatcher and the Conservative Party that the sheer horror of the Winter of Discontent and the clear inability of the Callaghan Government to do anything but plead for surrender terms, kept the spotlight firmly on Labour's failings rather than Conservative policies. The truth was that the battle for the soul, culture and politics of the Conservative Party which had begun with the election of Margaret Thatcher as Leader had yet to be decided.

The left of the Party was largely the wealthy patrician wing; the Thatcherian followers were mostly the more middle class new-comers in Parliament, and the lower middle class and working class grass roots Party members and Conservative voters. In the Shadow Cabinet and the left of the Parliamentary Party, Thatcher was accepted under sufferance, patronized and regarded as a passing phenomenon, an aberration which would soon pass leaving polit-ical business to go on as usual.

It is often remarked that her first manifesto in 1979 was middle of the road with little of the radicalism which was to follow, but that was more a mark of her insecurity than of any lack of radical instincts. What radicalism there was in her Opposition years emanated largely from the Centre for Policy Studies. Inspired by Keith Joseph after the fall of the Heath Government in 1974, the CPS worked in uneasy partnership (or rivalry) with the Conserv-ative Research Department. Under the leadership of Chris Patten, the CRD still looked to the memory of R. A. Butler for its in-spiration and the intellectual, cultural and policy conflicts between the two institutions reflected those in the Party at large.

Had Margaret Thatcher not won the election of 1979 the Conservative Party might well have lapsed back into the search for consensus, with a discontented right wing parliamentary rump and an uninspired party in the country. Once in No 10, however, everything was changed. A Prime Minister has two huge assets denied to an Opposition leader – the power of patronage and the intellectual fire-power of the civil service. The latter cannot do a political party's thinking for it but it will scrutinize and put administrative or legislative muscle on to the skeleton of party policy. As to patronage, there is little comparison between the value placed upon a seat in the Cabinet and one in the Shadow Cabinet.

Together with the other eighty or so ministerial posts, such patronage can have a profound effect upon the balance of opinion in the Party. Even more important, office gives the chance to test ideas with reality – a test whose outcome inevitably colours the fate of the Government and the prevailing culture of the Party.

Inevitably, just as she balanced her original Shadow Cabinet with due respect to her former colleagues in Ted Heath's Cabinet, so her first Cabinet was largely its shadow given substance. However, by September 1981 Margaret Thatcher was strong enough to drop Ian Gilmour, Mark Carlisle and Christopher Soames, bringing in three of her own supporters, Nigel Lawson, Cecil Parkinson and myself. Just over six months later, Argentina invaded the Falkland Islands. Ten weeks later, the islands were liberated after one of the best planned and executed and most daring amphibious military operations ever attempted.

Margaret Thatcher was no longer just a British politician. She had become a world figure and had sufficient political credit in the bank to give her the means to change the culture of the Conservative Party and even that of the country. Within the Party the defeatist attitudes that had dominated its leadership for years were discredited. It was possible to govern without the agreement of the trades union bosses. My own labour law reforms were being driven through Parliament. Britain could act unilaterally to defend her interests and British subjects, even those living at the other end of the world.

In America, President Reagan had assumed office in January 1981 and the stage was set for the collapse of the Soviet Empire, the end of the Cold War and the defeat of communism. The 'historical inevitability' of leftward political change was soon to be exposed as the myth it had always been. The consensus doctrine that the only functions of a Conservative Government were to smooth down the rough edges of socialism and improve the working of state industry was discarded by the mid-1980s.

Whether Margaret Thatcher would have won the 1983 election without the Falklands War is an interesting but irrelevant question. The war was of General Galtieri's doing. Her victory was of her own making and it catapulted her into the consciousness of the world. Although unemployment was still desperately high at the time of the General Election of 1983, a campaign led by Cecil Parkinson as Party Chairman, and myself as Secretary of State for Employment, was changing minds on who was to blame. Those blaming the Government were diminishing, whilst those blaming world conditions or the unions were increasing, and inflation was beginning to be seen as a consequence of governments' monetary policy.

The combination of Margaret Thatcher's international standing, her success as a war leader, and the greater realism and understanding of the causes of Britain's poor economic performance led the Conservative Party to a stunning success in the General Election of 1983. The culture of the Party was now changing from the guilt-ridden, consensual, apologetic acceptance of the 'left only' political ratchet to a positive 'can do' attitude.

The election of Ronald Reagan as US President in 1980 compounded the change. Under their leadership the policy of the West changed from mere containment and deterrence to positive pressure to end the Soviet threat. The sale of council houses began to widen home ownership, widening the ownership of a capital asset to a broad swathe of formerly Labour-inclined council tenants. The beginnings of the privatization programme – and particularly that of British Telecommunications – brought far wider share ownership. However much union leaders railed against (and the old patrician Tory left moaned against) these sales, union members and many Labour voters queued up to take part.

As one Labour Member of Parliament said to me, 'there has been a revolution and we didn't see it coming'. The hard left now had only one card remaining – the National Union of Mineworkers.

Mr Scargill called a national strike on 5th March 1984, but unlike Mr Heath a decade earlier, Mrs Thatcher was ready. On 3rd March 1985, as the drift back to work accelerated to a steady stream, the strike was called off. The new industrial relations legislation had prevented secondary action and without it the strike had failed. In the meantime in October 1984 Mrs Thatcher had survived unharmed the IRA/Sinn Fein bomb attack at the Grand Hotel, Brighton.

The Tory Party now had a true hero. Not only was she a hero at home but she was seen as a hero abroad. The burgeoning numbers of lower middle class and skilled working class families enjoying overseas holidays basked not only in the foreign sunshine but the reflected prestige of Margaret Thatcher.

A new generation of Conservatives were arriving in the House of Commons. The knights from the shires were disappearing and by 1987 they had all but gone. The change was not all for the best as Margaret Thatcher was to discover in 1990. Too many of the newcomers saw politics as a career with an expectation of a pro-motion ladder leading to high office, and too few had the public service ethos of earlier generations. Almost none had seen military service in time of war and as ambition was growing, loyalty dimin-ished.

The new culture had grown out of success, national and inter-national success, industrial, commercial and personal success, and it had to be fed by personal success. There was change at the grass roots but it was far slower and far less. Few local party members or elected officers were ever in politics for fame or gain. The long tradition of seeking election to local authorities to serve (even if sometimes a touch self-serving) was not yet touched by the cancer of 'expenses' amounting to salaries. However, the decline of locally owned businesses and the rise of national or international firms was exerting a pressure of its own. The middle income middle classes who would once have been rooted locally by their professional or business life had become more mobile as managers climbing corporate ladders. The politicization of local government and the vastly more varied social lifestyles lessened the attraction of party membership for the average Conservative voter who is not, of course, an activist political animal.

Conservative Central Office was shrinking in numbers and the longer the party was in office its influence became less. Party membership tends to grow in opposition and decline in government, and fewer and fewer local Conservative Associations were able to afford to employ the qualified party agents who were traditionally the links between the grass roots and Central Office. Several Party Chairmen, Cecil Parkinson and I included, had tried to establish a national data base of party membership, but without outstanding success although it would have clearly given Central Office greater ability to influence (and be influenced by) the local party membership. Paradoxically, Central Office was prone to feel to some extent excluded from the Thatcherian success story except during election campaigns. It lost influence and confidence and by 1990 was contributing less to the culture of the Party than a decade earlier.

Towards the end of Margaret Thatcher's leadership two issues began to undermine the success of her earlier years, and the unity which it had built. On the European issue the grass roots were becoming steadily more Eurosceptic and concerned at the federalist agenda promoted by Brussels. Although that accorded with Mrs Thatcher's own feelings, her inability to change the European Union as she and they wanted was a blow to her image. So, too, was the bungled introduction of the Community Charge.

The culture of the Conservative Party had changed during Margaret Thatcher's leadership, but not all of the change survived her fall, nor was it all of her making.

The Parliamentary Party had become in its composition far more socially representative of the country, but paradoxically at times far less able to represent the country than the knights from the shires. The Commons as a whole had changed. It had become a salaried professional business seeking the status of offices, office hours and staff. In the immortal words of Julian Amery they had

interpreted their role as representing Parliament in their constituencies rather than their constituents in Parliament.

Not only the Conservative Party but the world at large had
become convinced of much of Thatcherian economic policies,
and the doctrine that we all stand or fall primarily by our own
efforts.

In the same way, the greater tolerance of unorthodox lifestyles
had permeated the Party as it had done society more generally.
Margaret Thatcher seemed to regard sexual behaviour very much
as a private personal matter – unless, of course, it became a public
embarrassment damaging the effectiveness of her Ministers.

Perhaps above all she changed the Conservatives from a divided,
under-confident Party fighting only a half-hearted rearguard
action against state socialism and managing a national decline into
European provincial states, into a full-blooded confident reforming meritocratic centre-right party defending a distinct national
identity. She promoted a socially more representative Party which
appealed far more strongly to many traditional Labour voters in
England.

Unfortunately there has been considerable regression since her
parliamentary colleagues sank back into division and failure. The
manner of her defeat at the hands of the very men she had promoted tore the Party apart. The failures of the Major years left the
Party culturally divided, insecure and unsure of its Thatcherian
inheritance. The grass roots became divided from the Parliamentary Party. Its misfortune was compounded by the arrival of a
Labour leader wishing to claim the inheritance himself.

Notes

1   This is so even after William Hague's reforms.
2   *Editorial Note*: This refers to a conference of the Heath Shadow Cabinet,
    at Selsdon Park Hotel about 1968 or 1969. It came up with policies to fight
    the 1970 election. Harold Wilson suggested the policies were 'right-wing',
    and dubbed the Tories 'Selsdon Man' in an attempt to portray them as
    prehistoric.

2 Britain restored in the world

Malcolm Rifkind

Most Prime Ministers, and Margaret Thatcher was no exception, come to office with a clear determination to concentrate on domestic issues. That should not surprise. Since the end of the Second World War, few General Elections have been won or lost on issues of foreign policy, and most Party Leaders have climbed the greasy pole by their skill or experience on the matters that most affect people's lives – health, crime, taxation and schools. Thatcher's ministerial experience had been limited to education and pensions; in Opposition she had been a Treasury spokesman. One irreverent back-bencher, when asked in 1975 what the new Tory Leader knew about foreign policy replied that she knew so little that she thought that Sinai was the plural of sinus.

In 1979 the national priorities were clearly elsewhere. Britain had just come through the Winter of Discontent; trade union power had manifested itself at its most irresponsible, inflation and unemployment were constant threats and national morale was poor. Choosing Lord Carrington as her Foreign Secretary was a decision that allowed Thatcher to concentrate her energies else-where. Carrington had skill and experience; his appointment was a reassurance to the centre and left of the Party that the conduct of foreign affairs would be moderate, consensual and internationalist. Thatcher instinctively deferred to Carrington who she felt had far greater knowledge of the world and of diplomatic concerns than anyone else in her Cabinet.

But there is one major qualification that must be made to this chronicle of relative disinterest. From the moment that Thatcher became Leader of the Conservative Party she attached importance to East–West relations and believed that a much stronger and unequivocal opposition to the Soviet Union was needed. This led to her speech, in Kensington Town Hall in January 1976, when she accused the Soviets of being 'bent on world dominance', and she advocated a tough Western response. The speech was criticized in Moscow, the Soviet Ambassador in London protested to the Foreign Office, and *Red Star*, the Soviet Army newspaper denounced her as 'The Iron Lady'. This title was, therefore, first used to condemn not to praise her. She was happy, however, to wear it as a badge of pride for the rest of her public career.

No British Prime Minister can be immune from foreign policy and, even in her first few months, Thatcher was receiving Presidents and Prime Ministers, establishing a working relationship with the main NATO and EEC heads of government, and establishing herself on the world stage. It was the Argentinian invasion of the Falkland Islands and their subsequent liberation, however, that established Thatcher as a global phenomenon and which transformed Britain's image in the world.

At first, the invasion seemed likely to have the opposite effect. Britain had been humiliated; one of its last outposts of empire had been occupied by a Latin American military *junta*; the decline and the impotence of the British Armed Forces seemed there for all to see. In the immediate aftermath of the invasion, it was by no means certain that the *junta* would not succeed. Thatcher did not come to an immediate decision to send the Task Force. Her first action was to get military and naval advice as to whether the recovery of the Islands was feasible. She was told that it could be done, but that success was far from certain. They would be operating thousands of miles from home, in a hostile environment, without any land base and dependent on aircraft-carrier support for any air action.

Knowing that it was possible to be done was sufficient for the Prime Minister. She made her decision, which was endorsed by the Cabinet. She never wavered in the weeks to come even after

British ships had been sunk and many lives lost. For the Armed Forces she, unexpectedly, turned out to be the exemplary leader. She did not interfere with their military judgements; she gave them unstinting support in public; and while she mourned for British losses, this did not deflect her will.

Public opinion remained robust. Both the UN Security Council and the United States of America provided the necessary support while the rest of the world looked on bemused at this gallant, but quixotic, determination of the British to recover the honour that had been lost by the foreign occupation of these sparsely popu- lated, distant and largely unknown islands. The one cause of significant tension within the Cabinet was whether Britain should accept, as the United States wished, some compromise with the Argentinians that fell short of their unconditional evacuation of the islands. Thatcher was determined to reject any such deal and, in the event, the *junta* helped her by declining to offer one.

The results of the total British victory were threefold. Thatcher had conquered in war and seemed, at least for a time, to bask in a Churchillian glow. Being a woman Prime Minister made her achievement all the more glamorous and her country benefited from her prestige. Secondly, the Armed Forces became the heroes of the day. Proposed defence cuts were shelved, while the aircraft-carriers, instead of being mothballed, were ensured a proud future in the Royal Navy. Britain's image as the country with the finest professional soldiers, sailors and airmen received the biggest boost to that reputation since the Battle of Britain forty years earlier.

The third consequence of the Falklands War was to put in abeyance the assumption that the United Kingdom was locked into a process of gradual but inevitable decline as a world power. Britain again was seen to be a country that was able to fight for its interests when necessary and which was entitled, by its power and not just by its history, to a seat in the Security Council and on other global bodies. It is often said that politics is about appearance as much as about substance and it was unmistakable that Britain appeared to have recovered some of its lost glory.

These achievements, and that reputation, did not do Margaret Thatcher any harm when she concentrated her attention on Europe. The subject was not one that had preoccupied her in her earlier political life. It was open to the new Conservative Government to build on Ted Heath's reputation and to try to turn the leadership of the European Community into a triumvirate along with France and Germany. But such a strategy was never likely to be adopted. Paris and Bonn would have resisted it and, in any event, no British Government was able or willing to make the concessions towards much fuller and speedier European integration that would have been a necessary precondition.

It was also inevitable that Heath's ejection from the leadership of the Tory Party would reduce the enthusiasm in the party for closer integration into Europe. Thatcher was the candidate of the right wing of the party and although Euroscepticism was far less prevalent than in later years there was a significant caution and distrust for any proposals that would further reduce British sovereignty.

In the event, however, it was not to be the drive towards political and economic union that was to be responsible for the first clash between Thatcher and Brussels. It was the Budget and Britain's excessive contribution to it that aroused the Prime Minister's ire and led her to demand 'our money' back. This was not just a useful tactic to win support back home; it reflected a deep antagonism to a whole financing structure within the Community which appeared to have been designed to benefit French farmers at Britain's expense.

The result was a three-year deal negotiated by Lord Carrington in 1981 which provided for a generous rebate. Her partners had hoped this would be a temporary concession but with her much greater prestige after the Falklands War and with her uncompromising negotiating tactics she turned the temporary deal into an open-ended rebate entitlement at the Fontainebleau Summit in 1984.

For a significant period thereafter there was relative harmony on the European front. Indeed, on the most important Community objective, the creation of a Single European Market, the British were great enthusiasts and Thatcher an ardent advocate. So much was this so that, in order to overcome French resistance to the elimination of tariffs and barriers to free competition, she conceded the introduction of majority voting and the elimination of national vetoes to force though the necessary directives and regulations. This was to cause her some embarrassment in future years though, in truth, the British negotiators were successful in limiting the concession to Single Market issues.

The British vision of Europe had always been limited to close political cooperation and the advancement of free trade principles. With the Single Market approved there was no enthusiasm and, indeed, considerable hostility to the much more ambitious ideas for Economic and Monetary Union that were favoured in Paris and Bonn. Slowly and probably inevitably, the British Government became seen as deeply hostile to further European integration.

The problems were exacerbated by Thatcher's personal style. She was contemptuous of diplomatic niceties, and temperamentally opposed to the search for consensus beloved of the Brussels establishment. When asked, she declared that she believed there should be a consensus behind her convictions. She recalled that she had won the British rebate at Fontainebleau with few, if any, allies and assumed that she could stop Europe in its tracks in the same way. Not surprisingly, this gave rise to resentment and anger amongst her European partners. The resentment was mixed with a degree of reluctant admiration. President Mitterrand once famously remarked that Thatcher had 'the eyes of Caligula and the lips of Marilyn Monroe'. Rather less flatteringly, Denis Healey described her as 'Attila the Hen'. She probably took both descriptions as compliments.

Although much was achieved, neither Thatcher nor John Major delivered results on Europe that met even their own aspirations. The European Community continued on its march towards the Single Currency, the Social Chapter, more general majority voting and ever-increasing areas of European competence and policy harmonization. Neither Thatcher, who was emotionally hostile to the whole project, nor Major, who wished Britain to be 'at the heart of Europe', could prevent that.

However, the Conservative years were far from fruitless and frustrating. Britain led Europe on the establishment of the Single Market, had considerable success in promoting greater free trade in Europe's relations with the rest of the world, and was a champion of the enlargement of the EU to include the new democracies of Central and Eastern Europe.

Thatcher and Major were also successful in establishing an opportunity for member states to opt out of areas of harmonization that are unacceptable to them. This has not just been used by Britain but by Sweden and Denmark in relation to the euro; by Ireland which is not part of the Schengen Agreement; and by Austria, Finland, Sweden and Ireland which, as neutrals, do not fully participate in European defence. Firm precedents have, therefore, been created for a possible Europe *à la carte* which might, one day, resolve the growing gulf between integrationists and those who favour a looser union of Europe.

These years were also important in demonstrating to the peoples of continental Europe (as opposed to their governments) that there was a respectable, democratic case against a 'United States of Europe' and that one did not have to belong to the extreme right or left to believe in it.

In the last few years, the Blair Government, although supportive of the euro and the Giscard Constitution, has found itself unable to deliver a Franco–German–British triumvirate. And the divisions within Europe during the Iraq War have demonstrated that the issues needing to be resolved are far deeper and more complex than partisan comment sometimes implies. The future of the European Union is one of the great issues of our time and Margaret Thatcher, at the very least, ensured that the peoples of Europe, and not just of Britain, are aware that they have a democratic choice as to the kind of Europe they wish for themselves and their children.

If the Thatcher years resulted in a mixed verdict on European policy no such qualification is required as regards her impact on the Cold War and the West's relations with a rapidly changing Soviet Union. On East–West relations Thatcher's influence became substantial and her contribution was both constructive and highly successful.

It had not seemed likely that this would be so. When she came into office she was a classic Cold War warrior. The Soviets had invaded and occupied Afghanistan; their nuclear and conventional power, especially their navy, were expanding; their Cuban ally, under Fidel Castro, was intervening in Southern Africa. Many in the West were uncertain as to who was winning the Cold War.

At that time Thatcher advocated a tough and uncompromising hostility to Moscow. She was uninterested in dialogue and distrusted *détente*. When I visited Moscow as the most junior Foreign Office Minister in 1983, I was the first minister there since the Conservatives had come to power in 1979. That attitude began to change after the 1983 General Election. Geoffrey Howe, the new Foreign Secretary, encouraged her to hold a seminar on the Soviet Union at Chequers, her country home. I had been encouraged by the Foreign Office to recommend to Howe a build-up in our contacts and, in particular, to take account of younger Soviet leaders, such as Mikhail Gorbachev who might, one day, assume power and who seemed to show greater interest in reform. Thatcher was persuaded at the seminar that dialogue would be worthwhile but I recollect her making clear that, whatever happened, she would not go to Moscow. I remarked, *sotto voce* and a little flippantly, to Geoffrey Howe that she might go to their funerals, not realizing that this would be exactly what was to happen.

Thatcher also became interested in the reforms in Hungary, then, along with Poland, the most freethinking of the Soviet satellites. She was persuaded, reluctantly, to see Josef Marjai, the Deputy Prime Minister, and was surprised and delighted when he told her that the greatest problem for the Hungarian Government was to persuade its people that the government had no money of its own. But that's what I keep saying to people in Britain, she responded; and, in due course, she agreed to visit Budapest.

Gorbachev's visit to Britain was the first he had made to a major Western country (apart from a short trip to Canada). When Thatcher made her famous remark that he was a man with whom she could do business, this did not represent some starry-eyed revolution in her thoughts. By then she was aware that the Soviet giant was already in decline, the dissidents were getting bolder, and the communist economy was becoming known as having failed to deliver.

But Gorbachev also represented a new type of Soviet leader. He was young, good humoured and free, in his conversation, of trite propaganda. Unlike most of his colleagues he talked of his family, he was accompanied by his wife, Raisa, and he enjoyed, as did Thatcher, the cut and thrust of political debate. He remained a convinced Communist but he had convinced himself that this could be combined with human rights and pluralism. This was sufficient to persuade Thatcher that the West had to respond.

Britain, of course, was no superpower. The significance of Thatcher's conversion was that she passed on her thoughts and conclusions to Ronald Reagan and the White House. For the Iron Lady to be promoting dialogue and extolling Gorbachev had a profound effect on Reagan and led to a strategic change in American policy.

Thatcher and the United Kingdom gave full support to the United States in its new policy of constructive engagement with Moscow but, unlike Reagan, Thatcher never allowed her undoubted enthusiasm for Gorbachev to cloud or distort her judgement of how far and how fast to go. Reagan had committed himself to the Strategic Defence Initiative which was to develop a technology that would enable the United States to intercept any Soviet nuclear missiles launched against its territory. Reagan passionately believed that this would be a decisive means of rendering nuclear weapons pointless, and thereby lead to a nuclear-free world. Thatcher had no difficulty with the objective but took the view that any strategy designed to abolish all nuclear weapons was grossly premature and hopelessly naïve. In a tactful and diplomatic manner she made this clear at talks with the President at Camp David.

This, however, did not prevent President Reagan, at the Reykjavik summit with Gorbachev in October 1986, offering the complete elimination of all strategic ballistic missiles within ten years. Thatcher, in her memoirs, records that when she heard this it was 'as if there had been an earthquake beneath my feet'. Such a concession, she believed, would undermine the deterrent strategy on which Western and British security had been based throughout the Cold War. In the event the Reykjavik summit failed because of additional Soviet demands on SDI but the gulf in attitude and analysis between Reagan and Thatcher remained clear.

Thatcher's contribution to winning the Cold War was, thus, distinctive and not merely a shadow of the American approach. She anticipated and preceded Reagan in realizing that the Soviets were changing and that Gorbachev was the man of the moment. But once that process had begun she remained resolute in support of a tough, realistic defence strategy and was unattracted by, and largely uninterested in, theoretical initiatives that held up the prospect of a nuclear-free world.

On only one serious matter did her strategic judgement fail her. Her antipathy to Germany, because of its past, encouraged her to indulge a fruitless attempt to prevent German reunification after the fall of the Berlin Wall. She seemed unable to understand why the disappearance of East Germany was both historically inevitable and morally justified. But that error does not diminish the historic importance of the wider contribution that Britain, led by her, made to the most momentous achievements of the late twentieth century.

It may be appropriate to consider the nature of the Anglo-American special relationship during the Thatcher–Major years compared with the policy pursued by Tony Blair since 1997. Blair has been criticized not for being close to the United States but for allowing his support for President Bush to appear unconditional. This has been most apparent in relation to Iraq but has also been evident in his *volte-face* on the Israeli–Palestinian road map when Bush endorsed Israeli settlements, and on the 'war against terror' and its implications for civil liberties.

Thatcher, despite her closeness to Reagan, never faced the accusation of being the President's 'poodle'. It is not hard to see why. When she disagreed with US policy she made little secret of it. Thus when the Americans invaded Grenada, a country that had the British Queen as its Head of State, without any prior consultation with London, the British Prime Minister did not pull her punches. She not only had a furious exchange with Reagan which is recorded in his memoirs. She went on the BBC World Service and declared 'We in the Western countries, in the Western democracies, use our force to defend our way of life. We do not use it to walk into other people's countries, independent sovereign territories . . . If you are pronouncing a new law that wherever Communism reigns against the will of the people . . . there the United States shall enter, we are going to have really terrible wars in the world.'

She was equally blunt when Washington tried to bully European countries into ceasing to trade with the Soviet Union over the gas pipeline that was being constructed to carry Siberian gas to Western Europe. She made clear to the Americans that it was none of their business with whom Britain traded.

During the Bosnian conflict, John Major had similar disagreements with President Clinton over the use of air power against the Bosnian Serbs. There too, the disagreements were public but no lasting damage was done to US–UK relations. Indeed at the height of the disputes over Bosnia, I secured the agreement of the US Defence Secretary to sell cruise missiles to Britain despite their unwillingness to sell them to anyone else. At the same time Washington was trying to persuade Douglas Hurd to become NATO Secretary-General despite Hurd having been one of the main architects of the European policy on Bosnia.

Blair is too inexperienced to realize that the Americans are big enough to accept candid disagreement from known friends without serious damage being done to our basic relationship.

The eighteen years of Conservative Government from 1979 to 1997 happened to coincide with some of the most revolutionary changes in European history since the French Revolution. The fact that the United Kingdom was a significant participant and not merely an observer in these events is to the credit of that Government and of Margaret Thatcher in particular.

There had been no original strategy for a more active foreign policy. Major events such as the Falklands War, the collapse of the Berlin Wall and the Iraqi invasion of Kuwait were not predicted, and the British Government, like so many others, was catapulted by events into an interventionist response.

Sometimes, that response was ill-considered. On South African apartheid it was reasonable for the British Government to question whether sanctions and isolation were the best means of forcing the pace of change. But Thatcher deliberately adopted a confrontational and contemptuous tone with the Commonwealth colleagues with whom she disagreed. Genuine differences were exacerbated and unnecessary damage was done to the Commonwealth. On Europe, too, no emollient could have concealed the deep differences between British and Continental aspirations as to the future of the Community but Thatcher's hectoring manner made the inevitable compromises more rather than less difficult.

These defects were modest, however, compared to the positive achievements of her decade in power. The Falklands War not only repulsed an obnoxious dictatorship but restored the United Kingdom's reputation throughout the world as a significant power with professional armed forces that won their wars.

Her contribution on East–West relations showed a high degree of statesmanship. She put aside her original prejudices to develop a strong working relationship with Gorbachev, but she did not allow her genuine admiration for him to lead her to endorse naïve or utopian policies on either arms control or wider Western strategy.

Her relationship with American Presidents was warm and supportive but, unlike Blair, she did not hesitate to criticize, in public as well as in private, when she felt that the United States was being unreasonable or acting contrary to basic British interests.

The Thatcher years led to the British people feeling prouder, more confident and more relaxed as to their role in the world. For many years after 1945 Britain had seemed locked into inevitable decline through a combination of international weakness and economic malaise. Under Thatcher the so-called 'British Disease' became transformed into the 'British Example'. It is, perhaps, a bit un-British to expect people to rejoice at such a change. But it has been good, for both Britain and the world, that it happened.

———•◆•———

Comment

George P. Shultz

Margaret Thatcher, as Prime Minister and as a personal force, had a major influence on the strategy that ended the Cold War and on the implementation of that strategy. Ronald Reagan respected her judgement and sought her views, as did I. I learned that she liked a good argument and that she took her own advice: 'Don't Go Wobbly'. I salute her.

3 Britain and Europe: repenting at leisure

Christopher Booker

It is hardly a secret that the issue of 'Europe' played a hugely important part in Margaret Thatcher's premiership, not least in the events which surrounded her eventual downfall in 1990. But the very significant subtleties of Mrs Thatcher's changing attitudes towards 'Europe' have not been properly appreciated.[1] A clearer understanding of this throws light not just on the character of her premiership itself, but also on the damage the European issue has continued to inflict on British politics ever since.

The story of Mrs Thatcher's involvement with 'Europe' developed through three clearly defined phases. In the first phase, as a member of Edward Heath's Cabinet in 1970–74, and subsequently as leader of the Conservative Party at the time of the 1975 referendum, she was an unquestioning supporter of the official, Heath 'pro-European' line. During the period of Britain's application to join the European Economic Community, as we can now see from the mass of Foreign Office and other papers which have come to light in recent years under the 30-year rule, Mr Heath and his closest advisers were well aware that the ultimate aim of the 'European project' was to work towards full political and economic union (including a commitment to form a single currency by 1980). But they were also keenly aware that, both to Parliament and to the British people, the full extent of these integrationist ambitions should be kept out of view. Wherever possible, emphasis should be placed simply on the supposed economic advantages of joining a successful 'trading club'.

There is no evidence that Mrs Thatcher was a conscious party to these Machiavellian calculations, or even that, at this stage, she was particularly well-informed about the 'European' issue. One of her first acts after becoming Leader was, on 11th March 1975, to lead opposition in the Commons to the Labour Government's Referendum Bill. In this she echoed Heath's opposition to a referendum on Britain's continuing membership of the EEC, on the grounds that it was the sovereign right of Parliament to decide such matters (despite his pique at being replaced as Leader, Heath himself called her speech 'impressive'). On 16th April, launching the Conservative 'Yes' campaign, her remarks simply echoed the propagandist line being put out at the time by the European Movement, in its new guise as 'Britain In Europe'. She welcomed Europe's new cooperation as the best guarantee that the continent would never again be torn apart by armed conflict. It was a 'myth' that the Community was bureaucratic ('the entire staff of the European Commission is about 7,000 – smaller than that of the Scottish Office'). It was similarly a myth that 'our membership will suffocate national tradition and culture'.[2]

The second phase of the story began when she became Prime Minister in 1979. Already at the top of the British agenda was the contentious problem posed by the UK's disproportionate contribution to the EC budget. This arose from the peculiar arrangements dictated by France for the financing of the Common Agricultural Policy, agreed in the Luxembourg Treaty of 1970, and substantially designed to allow Germany (and later Britain) to support French agriculture. The nub of the problem for Britain was that she had joined a customs union which regarded import duties as a 'Community resource', which could then be used to finance the CAP (which then took up well over 90 per cent of the EC budget, the lion's share of which went to France). Because Britain imported more from the outside world than any other EC country, it was clear that within a few years she would be the largest net contributor. By 1978, when in terms of *per capita* income Britain ranked seventh out of the nine member states, this was already being described as wholly 'unacceptable' by the Prime Minister, James Callaghan. At her first European Council at Strasbourg in June 1979, Mrs Thatcher made clear that her priority was to sort out what had come to be known in Brussels as the 'BBQ' or 'British budgetary question' (or just 'the Bloody British Question').[3]

As is vividly recorded in her memoirs, this battle over Britain's payments was to last, through Council after Council, for five long years. At times her persistence aroused such impatience from her colleagues that this amounted to downright hostility (most notably in the famous occasion at Dublin when Roy Jenkins, as President of the Commission, recorded that West Germany's Chancellor Schmidt 'feigned sleep during one of her harangues', while France's President Giscard d'Estaing had his motorcade revving up noisily outside Dublin Castle, saying as he departed 'I will not allow such a contemptible spectacle to occur again').[4] Although, right to the end, the French continued to insist that Britain's contributions to the budget from customs duties should not be classified as a 'national contribution', Mrs Thatcher's insistence that 'we want our money back' gradually wore down her colleagues' opposition to the point where, in 1984 at Fontainebleau, they finally conceded the compromise which would allow Britain to enjoy a rebate. Although this was generally hailed in Britain as a triumph, what did not become apparent for many years was that the arcane terms on which the rebate was calculated, particularly as amended by Jacques Delors in 1988, would eventually inflict substantial damage on British agriculture. This was because, on various discretionary funding schemes, any claim for grants from Brussels would result in a reduction in the UK rebate. Determined to maximize the benefit of the hard-won rebate, the Treasury would therefore refuse to apply for those funds, leaving British farmers to receive significantly smaller subsidies than their competitors.

Although through all these five years Mrs Thatcher was widely represented as being permanently at odds with her EC colleagues, she continued to see herself, as she records in her memoirs, as 'a European idealist'. Once the budgetary issue was resolved, she believed, Britain would be able to play a strong, positive role in the Community, imbued with a vision of a free-enterprise '*Europe des Patries*'.[5] It was in this light that, in the months after Fontainebleau, she was keen to see steps being taken to 'complete the Common Market' by dismantling non-customs barriers to trade, in particular by supporting a report drafted by Lord Cockfield, her nominee as a Commissioner, suggesting how this might be achieved.

It was this which was to lead in May 1985 to the crucial episode which was to mark the turning point in Mrs Thatcher's relationship to the 'European project'. What we can only now see rather more clearly, from sources which have come to light in recent years, is just how little Mrs Thatcher really understood at this time of the real nature and purpose of the 'project'. In particular, she may have been ill-served by those whose duty it was to brief her on portentous moves which were being made during the early 1980s to reinvigorate the flagging process of the Community's integration.

Among the members of the first elected European Parliament in 1979 was Altiero Spinelli, a former Italian Communist, who immediately launched a campaign to persuade the Parliament to adopt a 'Draft Treaty on European Union'. This envisaged a dramatic new impetus towards political and economic integration, complete with a single currency. The Stuttgart Council in 1983, when Mrs Thatcher's attention was still focused on the budget issue, approved a 'Solemn Declaration on European Union'. This Mrs Thatcher dismissed as a document without 'legal force' couched in the kind of 'grandiloquent language' which 'had been used about the subject since before the UK had joined the Community'.[6] Nor did the British team at Stuttgart observe the implications of the commission given to another Italian MEP, Pietro Adonnino, to report on means which might be adopted to encourage the peoples of Europe to feel a greater sense of 'European identity'.

In 1984, while France held the rotating Community presidency, Spinelli sold his idea of a new 'treaty on European Union' to France's President Mitterrand. So ambitious was this proposed leap forward in the integration process that Mitterrand's advisers suggested it would need not one but two new treaties. The first should concentrate on 'economic' integration; the second, to follow a few years later, should centre on new moves towards political union, including a single currency. Thus was set in train the process which was to lead first to the Single European Act of 1986, then in 1992 to the Maastricht 'Treaty on European Union'.

All this seems to have been allowed to pass Mrs Thatcher by. At the Fontainebleau Council in June 1984 where her attention was focused on finally securing her rebate, Mitterrand slipped onto the agenda a proposal that a 'committee of experts' should be set up to consider 'future institutional reform of the Community'. This was chaired by a former Irish Foreign Minister, James Dooge. The British representative was Malcolm Rifkind, then a junior Foreign Office Minister. The minutes to the final report, presented to the Brussels Council in March 1985, show that the British Government, through Rifkind, raised few objections to the battery of integrationist measures which the committee put forward. These included not just completion of the internal market, but also extension of Community competence to environmental policy; significant extensions of qualified majority voting; and moves towards setting up a single currency, a 'homogenous judicial area'; a common defence policy centred on an integrated defence industry and a common foreign policy. These were the main ingredients which were to shape the two forthcoming treaties.*

---

* As Thatcher's 'personal representative', Rifkind was not authorized to 'support or oppose any proposal without the express agreement of No. 10' (personal communication). The countries whose representatives registered the greatest number of objections or reservations on the Dooge proposals were Greece (14) and Denmark (11). Britain came well behind with only four (one of which in fact proposed even greater integration, with an increased role for the European Parliament). The committee's final recommendation was that there should be a new InterGovernmental Conference to negotiate a 'European

When this was supported by Mitterrand, Chancellor Kohl of Germany and Jacques Delors, now President of the Commission, the scene was set for the famous 'ambush' of Mrs Thatcher at the Milan European Council in May 1985. So ill-briefed had she been by her Foreign Office advisers as to what was going on that she entered the conference room thinking the main item on the agenda was to be merely proposals *à la* Cockfield for the completion of the 'single market'. For this she was adamant that no new treaty was necessary. But, in an unprecedented move, the presiding Italian Prime Minister Craxi sprung a vote on the proposal that there must be a new treaty. Mrs Thatcher was outvoted by seven to three. She and her team were so stunned by the rebuff that they scarcely noticed a later agenda item on the report by Adonnino's 'Committee for a People's Europe'. Nodded through by the Council, it was this which was to give the Community its 'ring of stars' flag, Beethoven's 'Ode to Joy' as the Community's 'anthem', a Community driving licence and health card, and an array of other symbolic measures towards building a 'common European identity'.[7]

Within five months an intergovernmental conference, masterminded by Delors, had produced the text of the treaty known as the Single European Act. As its title implied, its real purpose was to move towards a 'Single Europe' by incorporating many of the Dooge committee's proposals, including significant extensions of 'Community Competence' on the environment and health and safety, and the elimination of national vetoes over twelve more policy areas. Despite Mrs Thatcher's last-ditch efforts, the text signed in Luxembourg in December even included a commitment

---

Union Treaty' (based on the Stuttgart 'Solemn Declaration' and 'guided by the spirit and method' of Spinelli's draft treaty on European Union, approved by the European Parliament). Britain and Greece proposed that this should be left to negotiation between governments for discussion at the Milan Council. In light of what was to happen at that Council, and of how Thatcher descibes it in her memoirs (which scarcely mention the Dooge report), it seems highly unlikely that its significance was drawn to her personal attention by her advisers.

in principle to economic and monetary union; while an intergovernmental treaty signed at the same time pledged member states to work towards a common foreign policy.

For the Commission and its allies it was a triumph. Mrs Thatcher had been so badly outmanoeuvred that she tried to conceal the full enormity of what had happened, by pretending that the new treaty really was about little more than setting up that 'single market' she so warmly supported. On this basis the bill incorporating the treaty into UK law, surrendering another very substantial tranche of powers from the Westminster Parliament, was rushed through the Commons in just six days, passing its final vote by a mere 149–43. Not for some years would it become apparent that one of the most damaging legacies of the treaty would be that avalanche of EC legislation – no fewer than 1368 new directives – viewed by the Commission as necessary to regulating the new 'single market'. This would in due course create huge problems for British businesses, without ever properly achieving that 'level playing field' which was claimed as its justification. But as Mrs Thatcher meditated further on what had happened, realizing just how determined the integrationists were on moving forward to their 'European Union' centred on a single currency, her views on 'Europe' began to go through a decisive shift. She thus moved into the third and final stage of the story.

The essence of the drama which was to unfold over the next five years lay in how Mrs Thatcher was to become ever more cut off by the drive to 'European' integration, not just from her continental 'partners' but from her closest colleagues at home. A first omen of this in 1985 was the surprising conversion of her Eurosceptic Chancellor, Nigel Lawson, to the view that Britain should join the Exchange Rate Mechanism. He had taken it into his head that tying the value of the pound to that of the strong Deutschmark would provide financial discipline and a corrective to inflation. But he was quickly supported by the inveterate integrationist Geoffrey Howe, precisely because this would tie Britain further into the integration process. When almost all their senior Cabinet colleagues supported them, Mrs Thatcher had in effect to use her veto to override them.

She then lost a Cabinet battle when her Defence Secretary, Michael Heseltine, another enthusiastic integrationist, proposed that Britain should join the Eurofighter project: a decision which twenty years later would emerge as the most expensive defence procurement blunder Britain has ever made. This was to be followed at the end of 1985 by the furore which blew up over the future of the Westland helicopter company. Faced with financial difficulties, the firm's directors had favoured a takeover by the American helicopter giant Sikorksy, whose machines Westland manufactured under licence. Heseltine was insistent, in the name of European defence integration, that Westland should merge instead with an Italian–Franco–German consortium. Opposed by Mrs Thatcher (although backed by Howe), he was so reckless in pushing his demands that on 9th January 1986 he felt compelled to storm out of the Cabinet.

By the end of 1986 Mrs Thatcher had made another powerful enemy. In the second half of the year, Britain held the presidency of the Council of Ministers. She records in her memoirs how, at the concluding European Council in London, she was irritated by the conduct of Jacques Delors, as Commission President, whose self-importance she regarded as inappropriate in someone she looked on as a civil servant. When, at the end of the conference, she took the customary press conference alongside Delors, she tended, as was her wont, to dominate the proceedings. Turning at one point to Delors for a comment, she found his attention had wandered and that he could not muster a reply. To laughter from the press corps, she remarked 'I had no idea you were the strong, silent type', a response which, according to Delors' biographer, left him feeling 'snubbed and patronized'.[8] This was compounded, soon afterwards, by an incident when she had a public disagreement with Delors in front of the European Parliament. She assured him that, although she had often defended his conduct in the British Parliament, she would not do so again. She was losing all patience with this 'new kind of Commission President', behaving like 'an unaccountable politician' and so clearly bent on building up the Commission's 'centralizing' powers.[9] Delors in turn was losing patience with her.

In 1987 it finally became obvious that the Thatcher Revolution was transforming the UK's economic performance in a way which, only eight years before, would have seemed unthinkable. Long gone were the days when strike-ridden Britain was scorned as 'the sick man of Europe'. In the wake of Mrs Thatcher's third and greatest election victory, she decided she now had the confidence to take on the corrupt, extravagant, inefficient, statist colossus that she had discovered the European Community to be, and to call it to account. As she saw the Soviet empire in eastern Europe 'on the point of collapse', she was determined to prevent the Community turning into another 'artificial mega-state'. She launched a fierce bid for greater financial discipline to be imposed on its budget, in particular to cap the runaway spending on the Common Agricultural Policy. It was a battle which was to last well into 1988, only for her drive to founder on the twin rocks of Franco–German refusal to allow any curb in agricultural spending and the determination of Delors to see the EC's budget substantially increased. He got his way, with a massive increase in regional funding which he regarded as essential to the workings of the project now at the centre of his ambitions: giving 'Europe' a single currency.

With the aid of Mitterrand and Kohl, Delors was now making his first serious moves towards planning this project which, like Jean Monnet before him, he saw as crucial to achieving the ultimate goal of full political integration. In the summer of 1988 a 'committee of wise men' was set up to recommend the best way to establish a European Central Bank, as the prelude to monetary union. Delors himself was its chairman. In July 1988 he predicted to the European Parliament that within ten years '80 per cent of economic legislation, and perhaps tax and social legislation, will be directed from the Community', necessitating, by 1995, 'the beginnings of a European government'.[10]

In the autumn of 1988, matters began to come to a head. In September the Socialist Delors won an ovation from Britain's trade union leaders in Bournemouth by a speech which contradicted the very basis of Thatcherism. His vision of the Community's 'social dimension' lay at the heart of his other key project: his plan to enshrine into treaty-law the array of workers' rights he called his 'Social Charter'. This was the moment more than any when the British Labour Party began its historic swing back towards an unquestioning commitment to 'Europeanism'. Addressing a Europhile audience in Bruges twelve days later, on 20th September, Mrs Thatcher herself issued a sombre warning that the 'European project' was now moving in absolutely the wrong direction. It was in danger of becoming an over-centralized, bureaucratic state, just when the peoples of Central and Eastern Europe were moving the opposite way in their opposition to Soviet Communism.

This, the most eloquent speech of her premiership, finally put Mrs Thatcher irrevocably at odds with everything the European project stood for (and had always been intended to become). She was isolated, not only in the counsels of the Community itself, but also from her most senior ministers. This was illustrated by the frenzied pressure she now again came under from her Chancellor and Foreign Secretary to agree that Britain should join the Exchange Rate Mechanism. Lawson, bizarrely, saw this as a way to head off the need for a single currency.[11] Howe, correctly, recognized that the ERM was only intended as a stepping stone to economic and monetary union, plans for which were now advancing by the month. On the very eve of the Madrid European Council in June 1989, the two men demanded a meeting with Mrs Thatcher, threatening that, unless she agreed to joining the ERM, they would both resign.

In Madrid, against all her instincts, she reluctantly announced her acceptance in principle that sterling should join the ERM, without specifying a date. On her return, she replaced Howe as Foreign Secretary by the virtually unknown John Major. Lawson's determination to shadow the Deutschmark led that autumn to interest rates of 15 per cent. As the country was plunged into a serious economic crisis, Lawson resigned, to be replaced again by Major, with the fervently Europhile Douglas Hurd appointed as Foreign Secretary.

As 1990 dawned, Delors proposed two 'intergovernmental conferences' to draft a major new treaty: one to discuss the launch of economic and monetary union, the other to discuss 'institutional questions'. The moment was at last nearing when that great leap forward to 'European Union' originally conceived by Spinelli back in the early 1980s could be brought to fruition. Both in Europe and at home, the pro-integrationist forces now saw Britain's embattled Prime Minister as the only serious obstacle left to achieving their goal.

By the late summer, with the inexorability of a tragedy, both events and men were conspiring to bring the drama to its conclusion. Mrs Thatcher was now so weakened that she had to agree to Britain joining the ERM. Delors was fearful that this might give the one leader who could sabotage his plans for monetary union a political lifeline. Therefore at the Rome European Council in October another Italian ambush was laid: two votes on 'political union' and the single currency, designed twice to leave Mrs Thatcher in a supposedly humiliating minority of one. On her return she faced almost hysterical abuse from the Europhiles in the House of Commons. Recalling Delors's suggestion that the Commission should be the 'executive' of a government of Europe, the European Parliament its 'democratic element' and the Council of Ministers its 'senate', she blazed out her famous response 'No. No. No'. This in turn provoked Howe finally to strike, first by resigning, then by the feline speech in which he suggested that it might now be time for 'others to consider their own response to the conflict of loyalties with which I myself wrestled for perhaps too long'.

As Howe intended, it was the cue for which her opponents, led by Heseltine, had been waiting. Eight days later, after a further eruption of mass-hysteria, with the Europhiles in her own party conspicuously to the fore, she was gone. As the historical evidence shows, it was 'Europe' which destroyed her. Her final major speech as an MP came on 20 November 1991, just before Maastricht, when she called for the British people to be consulted in a referendum before they were led into a single currency (otherwise they would have no chance to pronounce on whether fundamental rights should be taken away 'not only from them but from future generations, and which, once gone, could not be restored').

She had travelled the whole gamut, from her initial, wide-eyed acceptance of 'Europe' to her final, sharp-eyed perception of what it was really all about. But it was by now too late. Britain had joined the ERM, with catastrophic results. Her successor signed the Maastricht Treaty (albeit, thanks to her, without signing up fully to the single currency). The Conservative Party set off in disarray towards that wilderness in which it still flounders: without principle, without direction, without intellect and without understanding. In destroying her and what she stood for, the Party had lost its *raison d'être* and its soul. Our country is still paying the price to this day.

It would be only appropriate to leave her with the last word. Years later she inscribed her final epitaph on all these events in her book *Statecraft*:

> That such an unnecessary and irrational project as building a European superstate was ever embarked on will seem in future years to be perhaps the greatest folly of the modern era. And that Britain, with her traditional strengths and global destiny, should ever have been part of it will appear a political error of the first magnitude. There is, though, still time to choose a different and a better course.[12]

Notes

1   See Christopher Booker and Richard North, *The Great Deception: The Secret History of the European Union* (London: Continuum, 2003).

2   Edward Heath, *The Course Of My Life* (London: Hodder and Stoughton, 1998), p. 546.

3 Roy Jenkins, *A Life At The Centre* (London: Macmillan, 1991), p. 488.

4 Hugo Young, *One Of Us* (London: Pan Books, 1990), p. 187.

5 Margaret Thatcher, *The Downing Street Years* (London: HarperCollins, 1992), p. 536.

6 Thatcher, *op. cit.*, p. 314.

7 The Adonnino report is not mentioned in the memoirs of either Margaret Thatcher or Geoffrey Howe who, as Foreign Secretary, was sitting next to her at Milan.

8 Charles Grant, *Delors – Inside The House That Jacques Built* (London: Nicholas Brearley, 1994), p. 77.

9 Thatcher, *op. cit.*, p. 558.

10 Grant, *op. cit.*, p. 88.

11 So determined was Lawson on this course that, in March 1987, he had secretly ordered that the pound should 'shadow' the Deutschmark. He had not informed either the Prime Minister or the Governor of the Bank of England what he was up to; she only learned about it in November 1987, when she was told by 'journalists from the *Financial Times*' (Thatcher, *op. cit.*, p. 701).

12 Margaret Thatcher, *Statecraft: Strategies For A Changing World* (London: HarperCollins, 2002), p. 410.

4 Inflation, unemployment and the pound

Patrick Minford

At the end of the 1970s, the main feeling of those charged with running Britain's economy was one of hopelessness. Inflation seemed entirely embedded at rates of well over 10 per cent; 'incomes policy' was thought to be a way it might be contained but not eliminated. Any attempt to reduce it via a 'squeeze' executed through fiscal or monetary policy was supposed to produce an unacceptably intense recession with little ultimate effect on inflation itself. The central macroeconomic problem of the time appeared to be quite insoluble.

Yet within four years inflation was reduced to around or below 5 per cent where it remained for most of the 1980s, before some resurgence in 1988–89 requiring a renewed programme of action. The story of this period thus falls neatly into two sections: the defeat of inflation in the early 1980s and its final elimination in the early 1990s. The main focus of this chapter will be on the first but some attention will also be devoted to the second.

To understand the defeat of inflation, one must turn to ideas, specifically those of 'monetarism' to which the Thatcher Government turned for the solution to inflation; though there were two versions operating under that general heading. On the one hand, Milton Friedman (1968, 1980) had taught somewhat pessimistically that inflation could only be reduced via a reduction in the rate of growth of the money supply; that this would result in a temporary recession; and this recession could be violent if the reduction was too rapid or too substantial. Friedman's view was that inflation

expectations (which in turn drove wage bargaining) were determined by the experience of past inflation. Only once actual
inflation had fallen would expectations of new inflation fall; the
initial reduction of inflation must force down profit margins and so
drive wage inflation below what firms, unions and workers
expected to be reasonable at the time. Such a squeeze on the wage
bill would produce unemployment and recession, with firms
unable to finance both rising wages and current employment. In
Friedman's version of the theory, the fiscal deficit played no part
other than to determine interest rates. As the growth of money was
brought down, his argument went, there would be less overall
spending; attempts by the government to boost its own spending
or to borrow in order to finance tax cuts would simply raise
interest rates, given the overall shortage of money, and lead to
'crowding out' of the additional spending, with overall spending
being dictated by money supply alone. It was this pessimistic monetarist viewpoint that lay behind John Biffen's remark as Chief
Secretary that Britain faced five years of 'unparalleled austerity'.
Things, on this view, would be quite grim until inflation was
sweated out of the system by recession; only when actual
inflation had been brought down to an acceptable rate could real
economic growth resume.

A second version of monetarism was that of the British rational
expectations school at the London Business School (Alan Budd,
Terry Burns, Michael Beenstock, see e.g. Budd, 1977; Beenstock,
1980) and at Liverpool University (myself, David Peel, Ken
Matthews, see e.g. Minford, 1980; Minford and Peel, 1981). Our
view was more optimistic and gave a central role to fiscal policy.
Our argument was that *people's expectations of inflation arose from their
observation of the government's own policies*: these were to print money
at high rates in order partly to finance large ongoing budget
deficits. If these deficits had been financed by borrowing, interest
rates would have to be painfully high; keeping interest rates down
required monetary injection. Hence to reduce inflation expectations the government must reduce its inflationary finance at the

source. Once it had done this, market participants would perceive and account for the new factual situation and its rationale, and rapidly reduce expectations of new inflation taking place.

The Thatcher Government awkwardly tried to ride at once both these versions of monetarism arising from Friedman's revised quantity theory. The result was a big muddle at the start of the counter-inflation programme, as can easily be seen from a reading of the evidence to the Treasury and Civil Service Committee's Inquiry into Monetary Policy in 1980 (see e.g. Friedman, 1980; and Minford, 1980; both evidence to the Committee). The programme called for a simultaneous reduction of the growth rate of the money supply (gradually as recommended by Friedman) from its starting rate of some 16 per cent (sterling M3) to around 6 per cent over five years, and a parallel reduction of the budget deficit (the Public Sector Borrowing Requirement) from its opening 6 per cent of GDP to around 2 per cent of GDP also over five years.

However not much action was taken in 1979–80 to curb the deficit as it became increasingly swollen by recession; the full burden of this policy fell on monetary contraction. This was severe and much in excess of the gradualist recipe: what occurred was a very sharp recession in which severe liquidity problems in industry led to a large supply of emergency credit by the banking system, abetted by the Bank of England (which had no time at all for monetarism). This led in turn to an acceleration of the 'broad' (sterling M3) measure of the money supply which included the effects of swollen bank credit. Money supply measures not influenced by bank credit such as M0 (the supply of notes and coin) showed by contrast severe contraction in monetary growth. The policy appeared to be in total disarray by early 1981; there was plainly a very severe monetary squeeze and yet the favoured money supply measure was overshooting. Unparalleled austerity was in plentiful supply and yet inflation had been hardly touched; during 1980 it averaged 16 per cent, with wages growing at 20 per cent.

The major turning point in the Thatcher Government's fortunes came with the budget of 1981. Alan Walters threw his considerable influence into the rational expectations monetarist camp and engineered (in spite of Treasury reluctance) a very large contraction in the budget deficit at the height of recession. The idea was to signal to the markets that inflationary deficits were at an end and so to deflate the central force fuelling inflationary expectations. Meanwhile, interest rates were reduced and the monetary squeeze alleviated to allow the recession to burn itself out. During the course of 1981 the economy duly turned towards growth, and both inflation expectations and inflation collapsed.

What this episode showed was that inflation was really the result of the whole complex of government policies; it was, as it were, the private sector's way of coping with this complex. Remove the source of the inflationary complex and the private sector would quickly cotton on. It was no wonder that, as long as the government continued to run deficits in a misguided attempt to prop up the economy in conditions of inflation, no remedy for inflation could be found.

We may turn next to the other aspect of the 'British disease': unemployment. The recession of 1979–81 produced a sharp rise in unemployment – in round terms about a million (4 per cent). However, this was not the only factor at work. The Thatcher Government brought to an end innumerable props to the manufacturing sector's demand for labour: it removed subsidies, it removed credit support via the banking system, as the squeeze worked its way out, and above all it privatized the large manufacturing juggernauts dependent on public finance – including British Steel, BMC and Alfred Herbert. Thus companies laid off manpower in the thousands; essentially what was going on was a coming-to-terms with the market forces facing manufacturing. Hence much of the rise of unemployment was the response to these forces, delayed by a decade or so of government intervention. The 'manufacturing base' turned out to be largely useless in terms of the world market. This rise in underlying unemployment (the 'natural rate') – the result of poor competitiveness breaking through – was added to the effects of the recession. It became apparent therefore by the mid–1980s that much of the rise in unemployment would not be eliminated by the recovery. This led to a search for other, non-monetary, policies that would bring down unemployment: to quote Keith Joseph 'monetarism was not enough'. Indeed the monetarism of Milton Friedman could not account for the rise in unemployment in these structural terms at all. According to it the natural rate of unemployment was more or less a constant, while such distortions as union power merely served to raise the relative wages of union workers, not to cause unemployment.

It remained to the British rational expectations school to develop a theory of the natural rate of unemployment in terms of government intervention in the labour market: the key idea was that as the government made unemployment benefits available with little sanction for failure to find work workers made redundant would be less inclined to return to the labour market and find jobs. A further strand concerned unions: unions, it was argued, would create barriers to the return of such workers by preventing the reduction in wages their competition would create. Thus returning workers found themselves squeezed between the availability of subsistence unemployment benefits and the falling value of wages in non-unionized parts of the economy.

It took time for the Thatcher Government first to understand and then to accept these ideas. An early report for the Cabinet Office Think Tank had a substantial appendix written by Alan Walters and myself which set these out in early 1982 – this subsequently appeared as my *Unemployment: Cause and Cure* (Minford, 1983), later that year. Union laws soon followed from Norman Tebbit's Department of Employment. These began to have an impact on unionized industries: however, in the short run their main effect was to raise productivity as bad union practices were phased out and they did little to increase the demand for labour in these industries by lowering wages – this was probably because in the short run union power was still sufficient at this time to prevent employers searching for outside workers (as later they did).

It was not until 1986 – when David Young was Secretary of State for Employment – that the Government understood the importance of unemployment benefits in preventing a rapid fall in unemployment. At an influential Chequers seminar in that year, Young first set out his idea of 'Restart', in effect a tightening up of the conditions under which unemployment benefit was provided (later, Restart paved the way for the Job Seekers Allowance approach to unemployment benefit). When Restart was introduced, the effects were startling. Unemployment literally melted as thousands failed to appear for the mandatory Restart interviews and just took jobs that perhaps they already 'illegally' held, and thousands of others were stimulated to look seriously again for work.

So by the second half of the 1980s the British economy had well and truly begun to escape from its disease of high inflation and high unemployment. Inflation was around 5 per cent; unemployment was falling rapidly and had reached some 6 per cent (from its peak of 12 per cent).

Unfortunately, there was to be a relapse as the 1980s came to a close. The money supply growth rate began to expand sharply in 1986–88, largely because the Treasury under Nigel Lawson ceased to target it and instead used the exchange rate against the Deutschmark as its main target variable, and soon after inflation too began to revive. By 1989 inflation had reached 9 per cent on the popular RPI measure and 7 per cent on the cleaner CPI one, known as RPI minus X. By 1990 the Government had raised interest rates to 14 per cent and in November joined the European Exchange Rate Mechanism with the apparent intention of bolting itself into German monetary soundness, once and for all. Facing such high interest rates again, with the ERM acting to hold them up systematically at these heights, the economy collapsed again into recession. It seemed to many that all the efforts of the 1980s had been in vain, a mirage even; the economy was back to high unemployment (no cure there apparently) and inflation was on the rise again.

However, this turned out to be far too pessimistic an assessment. When Britain was mercifully expelled from the ERM in 1992, the John Major Government was forced to reinvent monetary policy. It did so in the neo-monetarist form of inflation-targeting. Monetary conditions were tied closely to the progress of inflation itself, thus short-circuiting issues of money measurement and also forcing fiscal policy to respect the inflation limits. Monetary policy geared in this way closely to UK conditions, unlike the German monetary policy imported via the ERM, turned out to be highly successful in stabilizing both the economy and inflation. The years since 1992 have been something of a golden era: inflation came down and stayed down, while unemployment steadily fell, confirming that the economy's natural rate had indeed permanently fallen. The pessimists, who maintained that Britain's underlying unemployment rate had not fallen and that its propensity to inflate remained high, were confounded. In truth what we have discovered is that Britain does not like inflation, can easily control it and can also have a competitive, fully employed labour market. The key lies in sound monetary policy geared to home conditions (by contrast with what would happen inside the euro, rightly rejected by the Treasury through its Five Tests) and in a flexible labour market environment. The pioneering discovery of that key was clearly a major achievement of the Thatcher Government; the Major Government's later rediscovery of it after its unhappy European adventure was a reassuring sequel.

As we have seen, the years since 1992 have been ones of economic success. Inflation came down and stayed down, under the regime of inflation-targeting introduced at the end of 1992 by the Conservative Government. Growth in every year since then has been in the range of 1.5–3.5 per cent, with no recession for a dozen years. The average, at 2.9 per cent, has been among the highest of the major countries. Unemployment fell steadily from 10 to 3 per cent (on the unemployment benefit count) by 2000, remaining at or below that level since. Thus inflation-free growth, stability and full employment have been achieved; relative to

Britain's own past, only the 1950s could match this experience but, at that time, Britain's performance was greatly surpassed on the continent of Europe and by the USA. On this occasion, only the USA achieved a better performance, averaging growth of 3 per cent since 1992 (though its instability has been greater, even then, with a recession, zero growth, in 2001). As for the big-3 EU economies, their performance has been abysmal. Though inflation has been low, average growth has been extremely poor (1 per cent in Germany, 1.2 per cent Italy, 1.8 per cent France). Unemployment has hovered around double digits (with employment ratios worse than this would seem to indicate), and recessions have been frequent.

Three questions arise from this absolute and relative performance of the UK since 1992:

1. What was its cause or causes?
2. What contribution was made by the Labour Government which held office from 1997?
3. What caused the problems in the major continental EU economies, and in particular what was the role of the euro (introduced in January 1999)?

1. The causes of Britain's golden years post-1992

The basic thesis of this chapter is that the groundwork for success post-1992 was laid by the reforms of the 1980s and the introduction in the early 1990s of the inflation-targeting regime. This needs to be considered in two dimensions: the control of inflation and monetary policy on the one hand, and supply-side policy – essentially the liberalization of product and labour markets – on the other.

The story of monetary policy has already been told. Monetary economists now understand reasonably well why inflation targeting was a successful successor in keeping inflation down, after monetary targeting had caused its basic defeat. The targeting of the money supply and behind it the control of budget deficits was used in most major countries during the 1980s to break the inflationary cycle; the UK was a pioneer in this policy, and similar policies were followed in the US and in continental Europe (led by Germany). However once inflation was brought down, governments and central banks discovered that money supply control (assuming stable public finances) was insufficiently precise a tool to deliver stable, low inflation because of the relative instability of the velocity of money. By moving to inflation-targeting they were in effect adjusting money supply growth for this variability in velocity, so achieving a finer accuracy of outcome. This neo-monetarist policy has been highly successful across the developed world; the one exception, Japan, proves the rule. Japan never moved on to inflation targets at the end of the 1980s; instead it followed a domestic monetary squeeze in 1989 (designed to end what the authorities saw as a 'bubble' in asset markets) with a regime of money-targeting. With falling velocity of money, deflation eventually set in.

Success against inflation can therefore be fairly ascribed to the inflation-targeting regime introduced in 1992. As for growth and the fall in unemployment, we have seen how supply-side reforms set both in motion. It can be seen from the subsequent behaviour of the economy that the period of stagnation from 1987 to 1992 was the result of a severe recession, the result of the monetary mistakes beginning in 1987 with the targeting of the exchange rate and continuing through the period of the ERM. The subsequent recovery made it clear that the economy's natural rate of unemployment had fallen to around 3 per cent and that its sustainable growth rate had risen to 2.5–3 per cent.

An important microeconomic aspect of these reforms was the transformation in the economy's structure from high dependence on (basic) manufacturing to an overwhelmingly service-based economy (with support from skill-intensive manufactures). This allowed the UK to benefit from the worldwide rise in the price of traded services and hi-tech manufactures relative to those of basic manufactures; this rise appears to have proceeded steadily since the

1980s and to be associated with 'globalization', as emerging-market low-wage economies have entered the world market for manufactures on a major scale (Minford, Riley and Nowell, 1997). By shifting its economic structure and trade pattern towards services and away from basic manufacturing, the UK too has experienced steadily improving terms of trade.

2. Labour's contribution since 1997

Labour is widely and rightly praised for its decision to make the Bank of England independent. However, the substantive monetary regime of inflation targeting had been installed in 1992, five years earlier. Bank independence acted as a useful consolidating influence in institutional terms. It also reassured market opinion that Labour would not revert to past inflationary policies (it was last in power in the 1970s, an era of high inflation). But, as can be seen from the behaviour of inflation itself, the essential change in regime had already occurred. Labour's contribution was to accept the regime and consolidate it, in particular against fears that it might be reversed (by Labour itself).

What of the supply side? Again Labour has been praised for *not reversing* many of the key reforms that had been introduced. It accepted and reinforced the philosophy of the Job Seeker's Allowance, thus not seriously disturbing the natural rate of unemployment. It refused to intervene in industry with subsidies or renationalization; and it buttressed the powers of the competition authorities. It refused to raise the main *marginal* tax rates, including those of income tax, VAT, and corporation tax. Broadly speaking, it also refused to roll back the union laws.

This list of negatives is impressive, coming as it did from the Labour Party with its history of interventionism and high taxation. But as with monetary policy, it represents a consolidation and absence of regress, rather than a progress or building on what had already been done.

Unfortunately, to the extent that Labour did pursue different supply-side policies, the record is rather unfavourable. Thus

Labour introduced considerable non-neutrality and retrospection into the tax system, when it financed its (ineffectual) 'New Deal' for the labour market with a windfall tax on privatized-utility profits and the elimination of the corporation tax credit to pension funds. It has worsened this non-neutrality since through a variety of 'stealth taxes' which have fallen in a haphazard and directional way on particular sectors: examples include now-substantial rates of stamp duty (on shares and housing), the infamous IR35 on small software businesses and the substantial differential tax treatment of small incorporated businesses versus large businesses and the self-employed.

On the labour market side, Labour has increased the business costs of hiring and firing, has given unions new powers to promote membership and strikes, and has introduced a minimum wage, albeit at a low fraction of median wages (and comparable with the USA's fraction).

This is by no means a complete list of Labour's infractions of the market-friendly philosophy it inherited in 1997 – see Lea (2001, 2003), Minford and Haldenby (1999). Labour's aim, under the dominant influence of Gordon Brown as Chancellor, has been partly to pursue a modern version of 'backing winners' (in this case seen as small and medium-sized businesses in technology sectors) but mainly to build up tax revenues – at whatever cost in incentives – in order to finance a very large expansion in state health and education expenditures. The trouble has been that this has involved reversion to the dominant-state version of public service provision; this in turn has caused a sharp deterioration in the productivity of the public sector since 1997, which has also been reflected in a deterioration in overall productivity growth since then.

Summarizing, we can say that Labour's record since 1997 has been on the one hand one of consolidation. But on the other it has introduced changes that have observably diminished productivity growth in the public sector and have at the very least caused some problems to the private sector – as yet not so easily measured.

3. Problems in Europe

A full examination of the causes of the stagnation in the major continental EU economies lies well beyond the scope of this chapter – but see OECD (2003). Essentially the problem has lain in the *lack* of the reforms introduced in the UK. This can be seen from the following Table 4.1 which shows some recent indicators of market liberalization in the UK and in these continental economies.

As a result, the natural rates of unemployment rose during the 1980s to around the 10 per cent mark where they hover today; growth has been poor because although productivity *per hour* has continued to be respectable, *hours worked* per head of working population have declined steadily. Finally, their industrial structure has remained largely unchanged and dependent on basic manufacturing, while the growth of services has been greatly hindered by tax and regulative obstacles. As a result they have been damaged rather than assisted by the worldwide improvement in the terms of trade of services *vis-à-vis* basic manufacturing.

What, finally, of monetary policy and the euro? Looking back over the 1980s and 1990s, European monetary policy – and in particular that of the big three economies – was set by Germany, with Italy and France acting as followers from the mid- to late 1980s by fixing their exchange rates fairly rigidly on the whole to the Deutschmark. German monetary policy was monetarist in approach during this period and as a result Germany never experienced the double-digit inflation rates common in the Anglo-Saxon world; German inflation had been reduced to the low rates that became common there in the 1990s at a much earlier stage in the 1980s. The same was not true of France and Italy until they fixed their exchange rates rigidly to the Deutschmark. By the mid-1990s the inflation-targeting practices of other central banks had also been adopted effectively in Germany and so via the exchange rate link in these other monetarily dependent economies.

Hence it was natural for these economies to think in terms of solidifying this link as the path to monetary success. Two main

Table 4.1: Indicators of tax and regulation

	UK	EU[a]
1 OECD index of regulation (0 least–5 most)		
Product markets	1.0	3.5
Labour markets	0.8	2.6
2 Unionisation (% of employees union members)	38	81[b]
3 Overall percentage of GDP devoted to public spending (= 'permanent' tax rate)	40	53
4 Employer social security contributions, 2003	9	24
5 All-in tax rate paid by employees 2000 (income tax plus employee social security contribution)	32	36
6 Total tax take on labour, 2001[c]		
Average income	22	40[d]
Low paid	25	48[d]
7 Minimum wage (% of full-time median earnings)	40	48[e]
8 Unemployment benefit ratio to net labour income (replacement ratio),1999	18	30[d]
9 Cost of establishing a business, late 1990s		
In euros	420	2333
In weeks	1	11
10 Maximum working hours per week	48[f]	35[g]
11 Notice period (days) (for employees up to four years' service)	28	50
12 Unemployment benefit duration (months)	6	4–60[g] 6–32[h]
13 Annual average holidays	28	33

Notes

a Average of three large EU economies.
b Collective Bargaining Coverage, 2000 (% of wage contracts by collective bargaining process; 32.5% in UK). Union membership (23% in these three countries) does not represent union powers of control because of laws governing collective bargaining under which union settlements are generalized across the parts of the rest of the economy covered by collective bargaining which is therefore a better measure.
c Difference between the total wage cost paid by business/production price and the net wage received by worker/consumption price.
d Euro-zone average.
e Average of Spain/Portugal/Netherlands/Luxembourg/Belgium/Greece/Ireland/France.
f Subject to voluntary abrogation.
g France.
h Germany.

Sources
1 – OECD (2002) *Employment Outlook*, Paris.
2, 8, 10, 11, 12 – OECD (2004) *Employment Outlook*, Paris.
3, 4, 5, 6 – *Forbes Global* (2004) The Tax Misery Index. 24 May.
7 – OECD (2004) Euro Area, *Economic Survey*, Paris.
9 – OECD (2000) *Small and Medium Enterprise Outlook*, Paris.
13 – Trades Union Congress. www.tuc.org.uk/work_life/tuc-4809–f0.cfm

possibilities presented themselves: adopting the Deutschmark or creating a new currency, the euro as it was named.

Adopting the Deutschmark would have allowed Germany freedom to set its own inflation rate and monetary policy to stabilize its economy. Other countries would have then had similar or faster rates of inflation, depending on their rate of productivity growth; Spain for example with high productivity growth would have had a higher rate of inflation. Average inflation across the Deutschmark-zone would accordingly have been somewhat higher than in say the UK or other countries adopting German-style inflation targets. But real interest rates in Germany would be set at world levels, while those in faster-inflation countries of the Deutschmark-zone would be a bit lower. While non-German countries could have suffered from the inability to respond to their own specific ('asymmetric') shocks, one can imagine that the advantages of access to the German capital market, of a somewhat lower cost of capital, and of low inflation would have been active compensations.

The adoption of the euro has caused a subtle difference from these arrangements. While there is an inflation target, it is decided for the *average* of euro-zone countries. This implies that inflation in Germany is rather lower than the average while that in countries such as Spain is rather higher. Hence the real interest rate in Germany is rather *above* world real rates, while it is somewhat below them in these other countries. Meanwhile the problems of dealing with asymmetric shocks are similar in principle across all euro-zone countries (of course each country's asymmetries differ in detail), with Germany suffering with the rest.

The main effect therefore of adopting the euro has been to reinforce the difficulties faced by the German economy. Not only can it not adjust monetary policy to its own shocks (recessions in particular); it is also faced by an artificially high real cost of capital. A modest part of the blame for Germany's poor growth performance in the past five years therefore probably rests with the euro. (For most other countries, the gains of low inflation have, at least in political terms, compensated for the greater cyclical variability they have experienced; of course they could in principle have achieved low inflation independently and without euro entry, but most found the difficulties of achieving a domestic consensus on such policies insuperable.)

Germany's difficulties with the euro have wider implications. First, it remains possible that if internal politics were to change they could trigger a German withdrawal – and the euro's consequent collapse. Second, they reinforce Germany's desire to 'solve' these difficulties by exporting 'harmonization'; this is a particular problem for the UK as a relatively liberalized economy.

The problems of the continent's major economies with growth and unemployment, as well as Germany's difficulties with the euro, constitute problems for European citizens generally. But they also cause problems for the UK in particular because of the consequent pressure from these countries to force an agenda of harmonization and EU-wide protection on the UK, as a way of alleviating competitive pressure on their own economies. This pressure has recently boiled over in the form of the draft EU Constitution which constitutes a major threat to the UK's liberalized market economy.

Our examination of Britain in 1979 has suggested that it was in the grip of an interlocking set of policies that produced high inflation, persistent large budget deficits, and high unemployment. In the subsequent decade these policies were discontinued: on the monetary side by the introduction of money supply targeting and sound finance and on the supply side by market liberalization, particularly in the labour market. From 1987 to 1992 monetary policy lost its way and exchange rate targeting was used, with the UK joining the ERM in 1990; this resulted in monetary mistakes and a severe recession which led some to question the effectiveness of the earlier reforms. However in 1992 monetary policy was shifted to an inflation-targeting regime which proved highly effective and revealed subsequently as the recession ended that the reforms had indeed worked well. Labour's policies since 1997 have on the whole acted to consolidate the monetary and supply side regimes already introduced; where they have attempted to be original the effects have been rather damaging. The main challenge to the continuance of the new regimes has in fact come from the European Union where the introduction of the euro against a background of relative stagnation has set in motion a more aggressive push towards 'harmonization'; in its latest incarnation, the draft EU Constitution, this is highly threatening to current British policies of market liberalization. Europe has yet to apply the lessons of the Thatcher market liberalization, while its premature decision to introduce the euro, essentially for political reasons, has complicated the tasks of monetary policy.

References

Beenstock, Michael (1980) *A Neoclassical analysis of macroeconomic policy*, Cambridge University Press.

Budd, Alan (1977) 'Disarming the Treasury' in *The Taming of Government* (ed. Arthur Seldon), Institute of Economic Affairs.

Friedman, Milton (1968) 'The role of monetary policy', *American Economic Review*, 58, 1–17.

Friedman, Milton (1980) Memorandum on Monetary Policy, House of Commons Treasury and Civil Service Committee, Memoranda on Monetary Policy, HMSO 1980, Oral Evidence given in July 1980 in Committee's Third Report, Vol. II (Minutes of Evidence, HMSO, pp. 55–68).

Lea, Ruth (2001) 'The work-life balance and all that – the re-regulation of the labour market', IOD Policy Paper April 2001, Institute of Directors, London.

Lea, Ruth (2003) 'Red Tape in the work place – the re-regulation of the labour market II, the sequel', IOD Policy Paper June 2003, Institute of Directors, London.

Minford, Patrick (1980) Memorandum on Monetary Policy, House of Commons Treasury and Civil Service Committee, Memoranda on Monetary Policy, HMSO 1980, Oral Evidence given in July 1980 in Committee's Third Report, Vol. II (Minutes of Evidence, HMSO, pp. 8–40).

Minford, Patrick (1983) *Unemployment: Cause and Cure*, Basil Blackwell (2nd edn, 1985).

Minford, Patrick and Haldenby, Andrew (1999) *The Price of Fairness*, Centre for Policy Studies, London.

Minford, Patrick and Peel, David (1981) 'Is the government's economic policy on course?' *Lloyds Bank Review*, April, 1–19.

Minford, Patrick, Riley, John and Nowell, Eric (1997) 'Trade, technology and labour markets in the world economy, 1970–90: a computable general equilibrium model', *Journal of Development Studies*, 34(2), 1–34; also same journal and title, 1999, 35(6), 153–5.

OECD (2003) *Economic Survey of the Euro Area*, OECD, Paris.

———•◆•———

Comment

Milton Friedman

I am a great admirer of Margaret Thatcher, but I have no expertise on recent British experience. I enjoyed Patrick Minford's chapter in this book. So far as his references to me are concerned, I believe he overstates my pessimism, or more accurately, since I am a natural born optimist, the pessimism of the implications of my analysis. Other than that, I have no objection to what he says. I have always believed that the most important thing Margaret Thatcher did was, almost immediately upon taking office, to end foreign exchange control and set the pound free to float. That was a precondition for other measures.

5 Property rights, incentives and privatization

Martin Ricketts

Historical events are subject to competing interpretations. The Thatcher Era reforms concerned with economic organization have elicited starkly different responses. A dominant reaction is that microeconomic reforms unshackled market forces with a substantial (even transforming) effect upon economic performance. These accompanied and encouraged wider social changes in manners, tastes and morality. Britain jettisoned its post-War experiment with big government and collectivist ideas. Individualism (somewhat narrowly construed in the epigram 'greed is good') was encouraged and the growth of the state was curbed and finally reversed. The Thatcher Government's premiership saw *The Retreat of the State*.[1]

According to an alternative view, the 1980s saw an extension of central government control over important areas of economic and social life. The scope for local decision-making was restricted and the centralization of the British state reinforced. Red tape and regulation continued. New regulatory agencies were created and 'quangos' (quasi-autonomous non-governmental organizations) proliferated. Passive exasperation in the face of bureaucratic restrictions rather than active entrepreneurial drive in the face of widening opportunities characterized the mood of economic agents. The Thatcher Era saw *The Tory Nationalization of Britain*.[2]

Both these cannot be correct. However, both can be seen as part of a larger more complex picture in which apparently paradoxical elements are resolved when placed against the wider background.

It can be argued that a recognizable liberal economic agenda was pursued successfully in the provision of private goods and the public utilities. In the provision of 'social' goods and services such as education or health, the use of true market processes made little headway and the drift to a more centralized and less locally diverse system of provision continued.

Two pillars form any economic system described as liberal in the classical sense. Privately assigned property rights to resources and the freedom to trade them are needed. Private property encourages the efficient rather than wasteful use of scarce resources while exchangeability favours the transfer of resources to the people who value them most highly. The absence of exchangeable private property rights reduces efficiency with which resources are used at any one time and undermines the incentive to research the wants of consumers, to discover new methods of production or to develop new goods and services. Entrepreneurship without privately tradable property, if not conceptually impossible, is in practice effectively suppressed. This has always been the 'common sense' and utilitarian defence of private property and freedom to trade, a case made more persuasive by the poor economic performance of those countries that were unfortunate enough to try out alternative systems lacking tradable private property in the twentieth century.

A liberal economic reform agenda is defined by extension of private property rights and reduction of restrictions to their exchangeability. The sphere in which resources are allocated by decentralized private agreements coordinated by the price system is extended, and the sphere in which they are allocated by governmentally mediated collective decisions implemented by administrative mechanisms is reduced. Such an agenda is also associated with a reduction in the burden of taxation. Most taxes weaken claims to property and are impediments to trade. Taxes on labour income discourage employment and encourage 'do it yourself', those on capital income discourage saving and investment, those on goods and services distort consumer choices. Only if taxpayers cannot reduce the amount they pay by adjusting their choices in the market will trading activity be unhindered by the tax system. The traditional liberal approach to tax policy is therefore that total tax revenue should be restricted to the finance of those essential public services that only a well-functioning state can provide. Further, for the economic liberal, redistributional enthusiasm is always tempered by awareness of the adverse consequences to incentives and efficiency. Thus for a given total revenue, the tax base should be as wide and as comprehensive as possible so that the marginal tax rate can be set as low as possible.

Economic liberalism is not a 'Conservative' doctrine. From the repeal of the Corn Laws in 1846 the Conservative Party has found it expedient to support free trade with varying degrees of conviction over the years. But economic liberalism is a system which always threatens existing dominant interests. If people have exchangeable private property rights and are free to come to agreements with newcomers or foreigners, they can always choose to walk away from existing suppliers or customers and contract elsewhere. It is this power of 'exit' that gives to economic liberalism its immense competitive energy as well as its socially subversive character. People are enticed to new products, new ways of doing things or new associations in a manner that offends the conservative mind with its respect for stability, continuity and 'time-honoured' methods. If the claims of property are usually close to the conservative heart, the claims of exchangeability and hence competition and choice are much more suspect and are rarely met with unalloyed approval by any powerful interest. This is the great paradox of economic liberalism and the reason why it seems such a fragile system even, or perhaps especially, to its intellectual supporters. The general social interest in the support of the system seems a weak force beside that of the powerful partial interests always undermining it.

It will be argued here that a tension was revealed between the claims of the liberal economic agenda and the necessity of constructing a coalition of supporters able to sustain the reform process. The Thatcher Government's response to this problem in 'political economy' is what ultimately gives some coherence to the apparently confusing and contradictory picture mentioned.

Privatization

By the late 1970s successive British Governments had acquired a huge portfolio of assets in a vast range of industries. The early years of the twentieth century saw the gradual advance of state-ownership. The Port of London became publicly owned in 1908. The Central Electricity Board was created in 1926, London Transport in 1933 and the British Overseas Airways Corporation in 1939. The post-War Labour Government acquired coal (1946), the railways (1947), gas (1948) and iron and steel (1949). Although the steel industry was denationalized by the Conservatives and renationalized by Labour, both parties added to the size of the sector in the 1960s and 1970s. 'Lame ducks' of the 1970s included loss-making car firms such as British Leyland (1974) and bankrupt shipbuilding firms (1977). 'High technology' acquisitions included British Aerospace (1977) and Rolls-Royce (1971). Natural resource assets included the British National Oil Corporation (1976) and a majority stake in British Petroleum. The National Enterprise Board was set up in 1975 to provide equity and loan finance to a range of companies. This was the heyday of UK plc, the creation of 'national champions' and the corporatist belief that government action was necessary to facilitate industrial reconstruction through tripartite agreements between employers, workers and the government. When the Thatcher Government came to power, the share of the public enterprise sector in UK gross fixed capital formation exceeded 17 per cent. The share of the state sector of industry in GDP was 11 per cent.

Originally conceived to be at arm's length from government (in the manner of the BBC) and with managers enjoined to 'further the public interest in all respects', the performance of the nationalized industries proved to be disappointing. Studies of the late

1970s pointed to the poor productivity record of state industries, political interference in their decision-making, their monopoly power, their subservience to trade union interests, their use as a key element in 'prices and incomes' policies, and their financial losses. The privatization of the state-owned enterprises during the Thatcher Governments of the 1980s was therefore of great symbolic as well as practical significance. It marked a new era. Political interference in business decisions can occur under private ownership, but the costs to politicians are higher and subsidies more transparent. Privatization is a means by which politicians can credibly commit themselves to leave managers alone to make business judgements. By 1993 the nationalized industries accounted for just 2.3 per cent of GDP.

It is significant the reforms gathered momentum slowly. Privatization did not feature prominently in the 1979 Conservative manifesto. This reticence is not surprising given the powerful interest groups ranged against reform. Trades unions had effectively destroyed Edward Heath's administration and the danger of exciting disruption across swathes of British industry must have weighed significantly in the formation of policy. But in spite of Margaret Thatcher's later reputation as a 'conviction politician' who relished the chance to delineate clear battlefronts, to force people to decide which side they were on, to challenge powerful opposing interests and to win, her success was in large measure also the result of traditional political guile and her fall came when this faculty deserted her.

Between 1979 and 1983 revenue from privatization was less than £500 million per year. The first large-scale privatization of a 'public utility' was that of British Telecom in 1984 in a sector experiencing great technical change and where opportunities for growth were most apparent. The gas industry followed in 1986. The water and regional electricity companies were not privatized until the end of the Thatcher Era (in 1989 and 1990 respectively). Privatization revenue exceeded £7 billion in the fiscal year 1988–89. It was not simply the pace of privatization, however, but the structure and methods, which reveal the influence of political factors. Worker and management interests could be accommodated through buy-outs in some instances or through offers of cheap shares in others. In the case of the gas industry, management interests were placated by privatizing the industry as an integrated monopoly and not disintegrating its production, transportation and supply components. The price of offerings was pitched at a level likely to attract wide public interest and rapid capital gains. Encouraging small shareholders to hold privatization issues was an important political objective. It made renationalization more difficult for any future Labour governments. It linked privatization in the public imagination to the creation of a 'property-owning democracy' in contrast to the system of nationalization which gave power to political and union 'barons'.

The Thatcher Government's populism and political skill in encouraging the private holding of property is nowhere better illustrated than in the field of housing. The sale of municipal housing to tenants was a massive exercise in privatization. In 1980, 31.1 per cent of rented dwellings were in the public sector. By 1990 this figure had declined to 21.9 per cent. Owner occupation had correspondingly risen from 55.5 to 65.8 per cent. As tenants, the occupants of municipally owned housing had the advantage of subsidized rents. The policy of selling these houses at less than market prices to the incumbent tenants enabled the tenants to gain the capitalized value of the implied subsidy in the form of privately assigned and exchangeable property. The 'right to buy' legislation was understandably popular. It increased mobility, it encouraged the more efficient use of the housing stock, it created rights that could be used as collateral for business or other loans, it improved maintenance, and the beneficial impact on the appearance of housing estates across the country was rapidly discernible.

The Thatcher Government's skill in creating coalitions of 'winners' in the transfer of property rights to the private sector was considerable. Fifteen years after her fall from office there is still no sign that this aspect of her legacy is threatened. In the case of the privatization of local municipal housing the main opposition came from local political and bureaucratic interests. This highlights one of the paradoxes of the era. To advance the liberal economic agenda, the Thatcher Government further weakened local political autonomy. It was not merely that municipal housing *could* be sold if that were the decision of the local political process but it *must* be available for sale to tenants. Thatcher appealed over the heads of the local barons to the population.

It was another local issue that presented the local barons with their revenge. The attempt to finance local government by replacing the local tax on property with a 'community charge' levied on each individual person had very different effects on local interests than did the sale of council houses. The Community Charge had some desirable characteristics in principle. Local people, argued the Thatcher Government, should clearly perceive themselves to be paying a 'price' for local amenities, a price that was distorted by the system of taxing the rateable value of local property, a varying part of which was industrial and commercial property and much of which was rebated to poorer residents. A more direct appreciation of 'price' might act as a constraint on local politicians and transfer attention away from redistributive schemes and towards more efficient administration. But whatever the merits of the case, the fate of the Community Charge indicates that Thatcher began to lose her feel for what was politically attainable. Far from improving 'local accountability', the introduction of 'capping' (centrally imposed limits on tax rates) and the removal of all local control over the business rates in 1988, revealed clearly her distrust of local political processes and her lack of faith in the power of competition between local authorities as constraining and correcting mechanisms.

Liberalization

The Thatcher Government seemed to like competition. In this she was an unusual politician. Even supporters of 'free markets' often regard these as necessary evils – useful in the pursuit of higher living standards, central to the inculcation of effort, a pivotal ingredient of efficiency theorems in economics textbooks – but otherwise regrettable. Thatcher's support for competition perhaps derived more from her love of individual liberty than from the pursuit of economic efficiency. Liberty implies (and the Common Law, by tradition, guarantees) that people can use their resources as they see fit providing they do not coerce or otherwise impede others in the process. Freedom results in competition, and the freer people are, the more competition there will be. The dismantling of arbitrary restrictions on rights to use or exchange property was thus central to the Thatcher Government's political as well as economic agenda. Many reforms can be seen in this light. In 1985, the legal monopoly of conveyancing was removed from solicitors. Similarly, in 1984, the Health and Social Security Act opened up the sale of spectacles, an activity that had previously been confined to qualified opticians. On financial markets one of the greatest of the Thatcher Government's liberalizing measures was the abolition of exchange controls in 1979, soon after taking power, a courageous break from years of restrictions and an important signal of what was to come. In the City of London, the so-called 'Big Bang' in 1986 established competitive brokerage fees after pressure from the restrictive practices authorities, and opened the way for the subsequent further development of London as an international financial centre. Rent control first introduced during the Great War of 1914–18 was gradually dismantled during the 1980s. After the 1988 Housing Act, landlords and tenants were free to agree terms on new lettings. Following the example of airline deregulation in the US (1978) the 1980 Transport Act removed all restrictions on entry into express bus services except those relating to safety. Before that date a single company National Express (a subsidiary of the National Bus Company) dominated the market. As early as 1981 the British Telecommunications Act removed the Post Office's monopoly in the supply of terminal equipment, a reform that led to new products and innovative designs for old products available through retailers of electrical goods and even through specialized phone stores.

The privatization of the 'public utilities' was a process subject to considerable political constraints as we have seen, and both the telecommunications and gas industries were privatized as large vertically integrated entities. Even here, however, attempts at 'liberalization' were made. The regulatory agencies set up to oversee the utilities were given a specific duty to encourage competition and the form of regulation adopted, price cap regulation, was designed to encourage new entrants.[3] Under regulatory pressure, the separation of the transportation and storage parts of the gas industry from the trading activities eventually occurred in 1997. Over the long term, it is open to debate how far the original intentions of greater competition have been fulfilled. However, the ability of today's ordinary consumers to choose their suppliers of gas, electricity or telecommunications services would have been impossible without the original reforms of Mrs Thatcher's administrations in the 1980s.

Of all the 'liberalizing' measures, reforms in the labour market were among the most contentious. The Thatcher Government's most famous measures were the restrictions placed on 'closed shops', the requirement that secret ballots be held before strikes could be called, and measures against 'secondary picketing'. In each case the reform buttresses the claims of the individual against the collectivity, undermining the power of unions to restrict entry into a trade or profession, increasing the costs of exerting monopoly power, and defending the individual's right not to become embroiled in other people's disputes. The liberalization of the UK's labour market has led to comparative industrial peace, greater flexibility and far lower levels of unemployment than are common in markets where labour has greater collective power. It is a tribute to the Thatcher Government's administrations that after seven years of Labour government these fundamental aspects of labour market reform remain intact and, indeed, are defended (thus far) against encroachment.

Public expenditure and taxation

The size of government as measured by tax and public expenditure as a proportion of Gross Domestic Product was brought under control during the Thatcher Government's administrations, but it would be difficult to show that there was a decisive shift to a smaller state. Total managed expenditure (which includes transfer payments) rose initially from 44.8 per cent of GDP in 1979 to 48.5 per cent in 1982 reflecting the higher unemployment of the time. Similarly 'current receipts' increased from 40.9 per cent of GDP in 1979 to 46 per cent in 1981. Thereafter, both proportions track downwards to around 39 per cent in 1990. The overall result – government managed expenditure of approximately 40 per cent of GDP compared with the 50 per cent that it had briefly touched in 1975 – was a significant achievement. But it did not firmly establish the UK with a smaller state in terms of its public expenditure share. Rather it located the UK in a mid-Atlantic position between Europe (France and Germany both have shares of around 50 per cent) and the US with a share of approximately 30 per cent. This aspect of the Thatcher Government's legacy remained intact until the turn of the new century (the ratio was still 39.7 per cent in 1999) but at the time of writing it is moving back in the direction of higher 'European' norms.

Controlling public expenditure is a thankless undertaking for any government. The liberal principle of taxing people at a low marginal rate on a broad tax base can still be pursued. The most obvious reflection of this policy during the Thatcher premiership was the fall in the top marginal rate of tax on earned income from 83 per cent in 1978 to 40 per cent in 1988. The so-called 'supply side' economists of the era argued that very high marginal rates of tax not only have hidden and pernicious effects on economic efficiency but might also actually reduce the total tax yield. Very few people paid tax at 83 per cent. Either they evaded paying it or they avoided paying it, and sometimes it could take several very highly paid lawyers to argue about the category into which any particular case fell. The top marginal rate of income tax is still 40 per cent.

Finding an easily measurable and very broad base for the tax system has been the holy grail of public finance economists for many years. The quest is beset with many trials, however, because whatever tax arrangements have evolved and however inefficient or unjust their effects, many powerful interests will resist changing them. One possible way of broadening the tax base, for example, was to tax the income in kind a person derives from home owner-ship. The stock of housing certainly yields valuable services. These services form part of the value of a nation's output. If the entire stock were rented (as was almost the case in the nineteenth century) the landlord's receipts would be taxed. In theory the case is strong. A significant increase in the base from this source would permit a lower rate of tax to be set on all sources of income. Mrs Thatcher, however, was not creating home-owners out of local authority tenants only to surprise them with new taxes. While she was in power, the home-owner was safe. The symbolic power of home ownership was more important than idealized propositions about economic efficiency. Or perhaps she felt that a broad base would simply encourage more government spending rather than permit lower marginal tax rates.[4] When change came to the taxa-tion of housing in the 1990s it was the mortgagor, not the owner, who was to suffer. Mortgage interest payments are no longer a deductible expense.

Self-employment

One important indication that the Thatcher Government's liberalizing agenda had wide-ranging social and economic conse-quences was the rise in self-employment that characterized her period of power. In 1979, self-employment was 8.2 per cent of total employment (the same as in 1969). By 1990 it was 13.5 per cent. During the 1990s the proportion gradually retreated again reaching 11.2 per cent in 2002. Something was happening during her period of office that facilitated this growth. The decline in public employment may have induced people to act more entre-preneurially and be more self-reliant, but this seems unlikely to be the entire story. Liberalization and privatization between them created massive new opportunities for the growth of the service economy. A more open and competitive environment and rapid technical change permitted a restructuring of the UK economy that had been suppressed for many years. Whether in finance, retailing, restaurants, entertainment, tourism, education or other areas of personal service, the 1980s witnessed rapid development. It was the growth of consumer spending on services during the Thatcher Era that created the background against which self-employment flourished.

Centralization

If practical politics constrained and moulded reform in the realms of privatization and liberalization, the same was true in the social services. Here, however, the Thatcher Government concluded that real market radicalism was political suicide. The National Health Service, Thatcher famously announced, was safe with the Tories. It would continue as a vast state-owned monopoly provider of largely zero-priced services. A reform based upon liberal principles would have renounced public ownership of hospitals and other physical assets. It would have used the price system to direct resources to where they were most valued and it would have confronted the issues of fairness and access to health services for poor people by systems of vouchers or subsidized insurance. Such a programme would have outraged public sector employees, consultants, and managers as well as unsettling large numbers of voters uncertain of the consequences and nervous about their likely position in an unfamiliar system. Mrs Thatcher's lack of radicalism in this area was therefore entirely understandable. Perhaps she also reasoned that she could not reform everything at once and that the underlying micro-economy was in some way more fundamental. While eschewing market liberalism in health, however, Mrs Thatcher did not actually do nothing at all. 'Reform' was considerable and involved the use of many confusing terms such as 'self-governing trusts', 'the internal market', the 'purchaser–provider' relationship and 'NHS contracts'. These terms were confusing because they introduced the terminology of competitive markets into what was, in essence, a reform of a bureaucratic system. The bureaucratic system was necessary to ration scarce resources between competing users without these final users actually confronting a price. Bureaucrats in District Health Authorities (DHAs) or general practioners (GPs), not patients, would have to face the 'prices' and their 'willingness to pay', after taking due account of the latest central directives, would determine the supply response from non-profit-making 'Hospital Trusts'. 'Contracts' between DHAs and the Hospital Trusts were subject to large amounts of interference and ex-post renegotiation. It is the sort of system that Mr Gorbachev must have been considering for an 'up to the minute' Soviet Union. When something has to be done, and the liberal alternative is unthinkable, it is this type of *ersatz* halfway house that provides a temporary refuge. Mrs Thatcher duly and sensibly sought shelter inside.

These reforms in the administration of the NHS had their counterparts in other areas. In education, the idea of the voucher made no progress under the Thatcher Government. Instead, by 1988, a National Curriculum had been imposed from the centre and schools were given the power to opt out of local authority control by accepting a grant direct from the central government. For the Thatcher Government the 'opt out' provision was a liberalizing measure, even a move towards 'denationalization'. It was an escape route for schools from local authorities that appeared to her to be oppressive and incompetent. Yet a system in which notionally 'independent' schools contract with central government for the delivery of educational services is not in the tradition of economic liberalism.

The state does not have to 'own' assets to control the allocation of resources. It merely has to have the power to tax and the ability to 'contract' with suppliers for the delivery of what the state has determined it wants. The great extension of the use of 'contracting' during Mrs Thatcher's administrations, a trend that continued through the 1990s and under the Labour administrations after 1997, is widely interpreted as an extension of 'market discipline'. Certainly suitably designed contracts can give 'high-powered' incentives and they can be awarded competitively. But the resulting competition is to serve the state.

In conclusion, the Thatcher Governments did transform the UK economy. Ownership of nationalized assets came to be transferred to private hands. The impoverishing struggle to preserve old industrial structures was ended. Liberalization and competition were encouraged. Public employment declined. Total and self-employment rose. The service sector grew rapidly. The growth of state spending as a proportion of GDP was halted and then modestly reversed. Marginal tax rates fell. Labour markets were liberalized and the trade union monopolies contained. There was a coherence about these measures that had a lasting and cumulative impact. Modern politicians, so fond of lauding the growth and employment record of the UK economy relative to others, base their success securely on the foundations that the Thatcher Government laid, foundations that most of them vigorously opposed during the 1980s.

Whether the transformation will be reversed in the foreseeable future is more open to debate. The decline in state-ownership seems secure, if only because politicians have recognized that state-ownership is neither a necessary nor a sufficient condition for state control. The liberalization of markets is increasingly threatened by regulatory interventions, many of them paradoxically introduced in the name of European harmonization and a more efficient 'single market'. Public employment is rising, as is state spending as a percentage of GDP. In the end, the liberal economic agenda is never secure. Its implementation will always be constrained by vested interests and its advances threatened with counter-attack. If the English keep Drake's Drum to summon up the spirit of that unruly privateer in case of further Spanish attempts at invasion, perhaps Margaret Thatcher's handbag will also be needed in perpetual reserve.

Notes

1   D. Swann (1988) *The Retreat of the State: Deregulation and Privatisation in the UK and US*, Harvester Wheatsheaf Press, London. Another book of the same title was S. Platten (ed.) (1998) *The Retreat of the State: Nurturing the Soul of Society*, Canterbury Press, Norwich.
2   Simon Jenkins (1995) *Accountable to None: The Tory Nationalisation of Britain*, Hamish Hamilton, London.
3   This followed the recommendations in Stephen Littlechild (1983) *The Regulation of British Telecommunications' Profitability*, Department of Industry, London.
4   G. Brennan and J. M. Buchanan (1977) 'Towards a Tax Constitution for Leviathan', *Journal of Public Economics*, Vol. 8, pp. 255–73.

6 The family versus the counter-culture

Patricia Morgan

Open many a commentary on welfare, poverty or social problems, particularly any involving children, and soon we are likely to find the ill in question attributed to Thatcherism.[1] Margaret Thatcher is damned for what she built or, at least, conserved, as much as what she purportedly destroyed. In particular, what she shored up was that awful 'patriarchal, nuclear, heterosexual family' – and all the abuses that flow from it. It is claimed how the 'ghosts of dead children . . . all destroyed by their fathers – smiled out from the newspapers . . . these children all died within the family, the institution sanctified by Thatcherism'. In fact, two of the children were killed by unrelated men and the parents of the third were unmarried and separated. Thatcher is credited with an agenda involving 'constructions of childhood, sex and sexuality', which included: 'childhood innocence and vulnerability; childhood as a prolonged period of preparation for (gendered) adult roles and responsibilities; the normalization and promotion of heterosexuality, marriage, parenthood and the family'; the 'marginalization of alternative sexualities' and even with establishing 'the link between heterosexual sex and reproduction'. If Thatcher was the market rampant, then the patriarchal, heterosexual, nuclear family is – at least as taught throughout academia – a handmaiden of capitalism. It is 'the site where the labour force is reproduced, both biologically and socially', and 'provides the setting for the unpaid domestic work and caring of women which keeps the cost of servicing today's and tomorrow's workers low'. Propping up this hatchery for little workers that parents would not otherwise want is social policy 'Materially . . . instrumental in reproducing and maintaining the labour force' and 'Ideologically . . . assists in the political reproduction of a working class'. It structures 'the patriarchal family whilst perpetuating the idea that the family is outside the state; a private sphere'. This sounds even more worse when you consider how education is involved: 'the syllabus and organization of schools help instil into children notions of gender differences and the naturalness of a particular form of family life. The Thatcher Government's concern with the syllabus is motivated in part by its desire to promote what is seen to be the traditional family . . . For example, s.46 of the Education Act 1986 provides that sex education is to be given in such a manner as to encourage pupils to have regard to the value of family life . . . a common authority structure in schools involves a male headmaster who is strong, paternal and responsible for physical discipline, with a senior mistress who is responsible for girls and who tends to discipline by non–physical methods such as shaming. The parallels with the stereotypical family are clear.' In all this, we are told that Thatcher was trying to put the clock back to Victorian times, to when 'crime was vastly worse . . . than it is now, London's streets swarmed with child prostitutes, and few places were safe to walk through at night'.

With a deep distaste for marriage and family life so often ascribed to the public, it is not surprising if those who appear to be offering it comfort are threatened with the people's wrath – as a sure-fire way for politicians to make themselves unelectable. A Thatcher effect or 'the impression that the . . . Party was extreme and prejudiced on social issues – asylum, homosexuality, the family' has been blamed for election defeats. It is forewarned that 'Great swaths of the country will never look at the Conservatives again as long as they retain their lingering resentment towards forms of social behaviour – single parenthood, gay partnerships – considered normal by most of the country.' The failure to support gay rights 'massively underestimated the effect that was going to have on the way people saw us'. To avoid putting off voters, the 'words "Conservative MP" should not conjure up' images 'of a middle-aged white married man', which appear 'mean, reactionary and out of touch with a changing country' – although Party strategists found that it was marriage which registered strongly with voters in their pre-2001 election *Listening to Britain* exercise. With claims that 'inclusion should involve dismantling the roadblocks which have prevented members of ethnic communities or gay voters supporting the Tories', what were the particular 'barriers' to electoral acceptability and political power which even 'denied them not just support but even a hearing'? These were listed as support for Section 28, a law of 1988 forbidding the promotion of homosexuality in schools, suggestions that 'the war against drugs should be fought in middle-class teenage bedrooms' and 'estrangement from the difficulties women have juggling work and family'. The election of a new leader has not stilled accusations that the Tories are 'grotesquely unrepresentative' and 'poorly regarded' by the 'public at large', by whom they will be duly snubbed at the polling booths for not giving 'single mothers or gay citizens' the 'respect they deserve'.

The Tories have now themselves bought into the story of their supposed grand plan to prop up the hated nuclear, heterosexual family, and how the road back to power involves expiation for such sin. In 'an extraordinary admission of its past hostility', the 'Conservatives declared . . . that the party's "War" on lone mothers was over', at the Party conference in 2002. So that there could be no mistake that the Tories accepted 'families came in all shapes and sizes', on the platform was Kate Green, Director of the National Council for One Parent Families. The Tories under Michael Howard have been 'keen not to tell people how to live their lives after the row over gay adoption under Iain Duncan Smith'. *Mea culpa, mea maxima culpa.* According to David Willetts 'the last thing that families need is politicians adding to the chorus of blame that has been heaped on Britain's families'.

But was a chorus of blame heaped on Britain's families – or

rather, was there a 'war on lone parents'? More to the point, did Thatcher Governments impose a hated institution onto a people anxious to be rid of it, and eager to be divorced, to be lone parents or gay? Did the people suffer under a regime which forbade divorce, abortion and contraception and discouraged the employment of women? Did Thatcher Governments throw all manner of benefits at married couples and at children with married parents, 'force' couples to marry, while cutting off welfare to lone mothers? Did Thatcher Governments preside over the upsurge of crime because they starved a desperate population?

When the European Values Study 1990 asked people in Britain if they agreed that marriage was an outdated institution, 81 per cent said no (17 per cent said yes and 2 per cent did not know). Moreover, 73 per cent said that a child needed both a mother and a father to grow up happily even if this was one of the lowest rates in Europe (Italy was 96 per cent and France 92 per cent). Most 'ethnic communities' looked as though they might be deeply unhappy lining up with 'gay voters', and had supported Section 28. If it was 'extreme and prejudiced' not to want homosexuality promoted in schools, then 86 per cent of people expressed a wish not to change the law in Scotland to attain this, and in England attitudes were similar. If support for marriage was bigoted and intolerant, then this described the 68 per cent of the public who favoured a special tax allowance for married couples in 1999 (only 24 per cent opposed). Instead of provoking disgust, it looked more as if the Tories had lamentably failed in 2001 to capitalize on such disappointed expectations, by proposing only that married couples raising young children might transfer their unused tax allowance to the working spouse (only 1.5 million married couples would have been eligible out of a total of 10 million, and 6 million of the 7.5 million families with children would fail to benefit).

If the policies Thatcher Governments are accused of supporting do not look so unpopular after all, what was the health of the family like in her time? As it was, the proportion of married households fell from 68 per cent in 1971 to 64 per cent in 1981 to

55 per cent in 1991 to 45 per cent in 2001. By 2001, 30 per cent of households simply had one person. Twenty-two per cent of children under sixteen were with lone parents and 11 per cent with cohabitees, even if 60 per cent were still with married couples – despite this group being treated as an irrelevant minority in need of 'modernization'. However, 'alternatives' were clearly growing apace in Thatcher's Britain. In 1970, there were just over a half a million lone parents. By 1996, this had become 1.6 million, with nearly three million children, as the proportion of households consisting of a lone parent with dependent children trebled. Only seven per cent of children lived with lone parent families in 1972, and much of the increase to over one in five occurred in the 1980s. Up into the mid-1980s, nearly three-quarters of the increase in the number of lone parent families was attributable to the rise in divorced and separated mothers, as divorce rose enormously after the Divorce Reform Act 1969 and stayed high. The number of children under sixteen involved in divorce grew steadily from 82,000 in 1971 to peak in 1993, with 176,000. As rates of re-marriage fell, this reinforced the impact of rising divorce on the number of lone parents. One in four children born in 1979 is estimated to have been affected by divorce before reaching the age of sixteen.

Births outside marriage also went into vertical ascent in the 1980s, as the one baby in ten born to an unmarried mother in the late 1970s rose to two in ten in 1986 and nearly four in ten by 1997 – overtaking the USA. Although the trends started earlier in the USA, the pace of change was faster in the UK. Around a half of first births outside marriage in England and Wales are probably born into cohabitational unions and, as the marriage rate slumped by more than a third between 1971 and 1995, cohabitations became less likely to lead to marriage. By the mid-1990s, two-fifths of British women having their first child in cohabitation were married within ten years, but a half were lone unmarried mothers because their relationships had collapsed. Cohabitations with children break up at fourfold or more the rate of marriages and even with economic and other factors like age and duration controlled for, the ratio cannot be reduced below two to one. In turn, there have been more completely 'solo' mothers who have never lived with the man, and more teenage conceptions (rising from 57.1 per 1,000 in 1981 to 65.3 in 1991).

The whole phenomenon has to be seen in relation to low marriage rates and the falling population of married people, so that births to increasing numbers of single women represent a rising proportion of the total birth rate. In 1971, 80 per cent of women were married by the age of 25, but in 1990 a half were single, and the number of males never married by the age of 29 grew from a quarter to a half. A result was that one in ten men aged 25 to 44 was living alone in 1994, three times the proportion of 1973. This general retreat from marriage accompanied a retreat from marital childbearing. The falling overall birth rate since the mid-1970s is accounted for by the decline in births to married women. The reverse applies to lone parents, where a growth in family size is concentrated among single lone mothers. In 1971, lone parents had an average of 1.79 children and couples 2.03; by 1996, these figures had drawn together at 1.73 and 1.85. Married women have children later than single women; fewer married women are having second or subsequent births and more have no children at all.

Rising divorce and unwed births, together with the implosion in marital births, mark the decline in marriage as a family-forming institution. The result is that, while 83 per cent of children in 1979 were living with two natural and married parents, this dropped to 68 per cent by 1991/92, the end of the Thatcher years. The accelerating decay of the traditional family unit and the relative paucity of children were pointers to developments that were eroding or undermining the capacity of the society to replace itself adequately. If this was the end result of a policy to impose 'the patriarchal, nuclear, heterosexual family' on one and all, then it clearly backfired disastrously, or was extraordinarily unsuccessful. But was there one at all?

Far from being driven into the patriarchal, nuclear, heterosexual family, women could 'marry the state' as the traditional male role was socialized – principally between 1979–90. In 1973 the long-term rate of social security (some 25 per cent higher than the normal rate) was paid to lone parents after two years, but from 1980, it was paid after one year – with lone parents doing relatively well out of the changes following the 1978 Social Assistance Review. The higher rate of basic benefit for adults (previously restricted to the old and disabled) was extended to provide an *alternative* to employment for lone mothers of dependent children. From 1988, the long-term rate was replaced by a lone parent premium for all, and those aged 18 to 24 received the higher rate for single persons over 25. Lone parents on basic benefit also profited from higher earnings disregards than couples – introduced in 1976, and later raised as well as extended to Housing Benefit and Council Tax Benefit. The accumulating 'passport benefits' attached to means-tested allowances covered free school meals, milk and vitamins for pregnant women and young children, maternity payments for new babies, free prescriptions, exemptions from optical and dental charges and travel costs to and from hospital, grants for school or education-related expenses, and concessions for courses, leisure activities and much more.

In-work benefits also gave a privileged status to lone parents. At its inception in the early 1970s, Family Income Supplement (FIS) defined full-time work as 30 hours per week, but from April 1979 lone parents qualified if they worked 24 hours a week. In 1988 Family Credit replaced FIS and in 1992 the working hours needed to qualify fell to sixteen. (In 1994 came child care allowances, where the mother might perform the traditional male role, while the state looked after the babies.) For in-work benefits, as well as housing and local tax benefits there were maintenance disregards, while all of a spouse's income counted against the entitlements of couples and no account was taken of there being two adults to keep instead of one. A couple's joint income restricted their benefits, whilst at the same time denying them any right to pool their tax allowances. From the late 1970s, there was also a universal higher rate of Child Benefit for lone parents (or One-parent Benefit). Where one person could achieve as much or more net income to support fewer adults then, at any given level of earnings, a married couple took home less than a single parent on the same earnings and with the same number of children. Analyses of child-rearing costs or the impact of the 1980 or 1986 social security legislation showed how unemployed or low-paid two-parent families were worse off than lone parents, and more likely to report financial hardship, debts and difficulties in making ends meet and suggested that 'targeting by the Department of Social Security is either carried out blindfold or is based on criteria other than need'.

At the same time as the benefits system was seen and developed as something for lone parents, so was social housing. Legal obliga-tions on local authorities under Part III of the 1985 Housing Act to arrange permanent accommodation for the homeless who fall into a priority need category did not distinguish between one- or two-parent households; lone parents qualifying for help in being both pregnant women (or people with dependent children), and '*people who are vulnerable* owing to old age, physical or mental ill-health *or some other special reason*' (emphasis added). Accordingly, the proportion of lone mothers living alone doubled between 1974 and 1989, to 73 per cent, as some authorities turned their responsibilities into a housing policy that essentially provided only for lone parents. Couples on the waiting list for local authority housing could improve their (otherwise almost non-existent) chances if the woman was pregnant and the man deserted.

As lone parenthood climbed upwards, so did the proportion of lone parents claiming all or much of their income from public assistance. The proportion dependent upon Income Support – payable to lone parents without them having to seek work until children were sixteen – rose from 37 per cent to over two-thirds between 1971 and 1989, as the numbers rose from 213,000 in 1971 to 1,440,000 in 1996. Dependence upon Income Support also became a long-term rather than a short-term phenomenon, particularly for single lone mothers and by the mid-1980s over 90 per cent with young children derived their incomes in this way. Unemployment and the growth of lone parenthood pushed the child population on Income Support to almost one in four by 1993, compared to 7 per cent in 1979. (The overall proportion of under-fives whose parents received either Income Support or Family Credit stood at nearly 40 per cent in 1992/3 and approached 30 per cent for children aged twelve to fifteen years.)

Unsurprisingly, lone parent benefit dependency meant big falls in the proportion in employment in the 1980s, when that of married mothers was on the rise. As the employment rate for married mothers with a child under five nearly doubled from 23 to 45 per cent between 1981 and 1990, the proportion of lone mothers in employment was almost half that of 'couple' mothers, and an increasing proportion had never worked. This has become a leading reason why more people came to live in workless households, and why the proportion of children living without a working parent increased from 9 per cent in 1979 to 23 per cent in 1995/6 and those living without a parent working full time increased from 18 to 32 per cent. Even when brought into poverty and onto means-related benefits, two-parent families exit sooner and at higher rates than lone parents, who accumulate.

By the century's end, lone parents were over twelve times as likely to be receiving Income Support as couples with dependent children (51 versus 4 per cent), and 2.5 times as likely to be receiving Family Credit or (now) Working Families Tax Credit (24 versus 9 per cent). More or less 60 per cent of lone parents received Housing Benefit and Council Tax Benefit, compared with around 10 per cent or less for couples with children.[2] By 1992–93, support for lone parenthood amounted to £6.6 billion, an increase of 170 per cent since 1978–79, and as much as the Department of Education spent on higher and further education. Its cost to the social security budget exceeded that of unemployment. All in all, child contingent support rose from 14.7 to 32.7 per cent as a proportion of total disposable income for lone parents with one child, and from 3.4 to 5.7 per cent for couples with one child between 1975 and 2003.

In the Thatcher Era, parenting outside marriage became the only form of child-raising that government seemed willing to subsidize substantially, as married couples with children dropped below the eyeline of policy-makers or were regarded as unsuitable or unworthy subjects for care and attention. Proper recognition and support for marriage could have encouraged the formation of marriages by women who might otherwise have become lone parents, and by men who would otherwise be absent fathers. The concept of the 'family wage' once referred to the various ways in which the living standards of married-couple households were sustained, as husband and wife covered the tasks of child-rearing through mutual support. Now there were 'packages' for lone parents, or the supplements and substitutes that enabled all the aspects of the parental role to be invested in one person, as the predicament of the mother and child unit dominated public debate. When FIS was introduced in the early 1970s, the client group was envisaged as the low paid, (often one-wage) family, perhaps with several children. In the 1980s, financial difficulties in the working-age population became 'lone-parent poverty' as the poor parent became synonymous with the lone parent. Crucially, this ignored the preponderance of two-parent families at the poorest levels, where they formed a decided majority in the bottom 10 per cent of the income distribution. It is the dramatic increase in the number of lone parents on Income Support in the 1980s which in part explains why 58 per cent of lone-parent families had below half average incomes by 1992/3, compared to 19 per cent in 1979. But then, it is also significant that the proportion of couples with children below half average income also trebled from 8 to 24 per cent over the same period.

Inequality grew and child poverty certainly grew – but the system privileged non-marriage. Entitled to long-term assistance without a work test and with housing costs paid, lone parents were relatively well cushioned from the tribulations suffered by the working population in the labour and housing markets. The UK saw a huge rise in the number of children living in relative poverty, as rates increased dramatically over the 1980s, more slowly in the 1990s and then stabilized or fell. The increase was nearly threefold from the 1970s to the end of the century, with the percentage peaking at 33.9 in 1996/7. Whatever arguments surround the measurement of poverty (which is always going to be defined relatively, as it was by Adam Smith), the fact is that families with children were increasingly likely to occupy the lower parts of the income range and to be more prone to spells of economic distress of a greater or lesser duration – even though more homes had two parents in the workforce and there were fewer children. Without the upward pressure on poverty rates exerted by more lone parents, it seems likely that a significant rise would have occurred anyway. At the same time, the increasing proportion of families claiming means-tested benefits was symptomatic of the decline of the middle and respectable working classes as the income distribution pulled apart, a process accompanied by the rise of a welfare-dependent underclass.

Child-rearing imposes considerable costs. It makes substantial and simultaneous demands in terms of money and time – money and time forgone just at the period when outlay is rising. Variations in living standards owe as much or more to differences in family responsibilities as to levels of initial income. In the waged economy, poverty is bound to be concentrated among those with dependants. Traditionally, the financial burden of raising children was much eased by a range of measures which protected the family's economic security, and which helped to maintain some parity in living standards between those with and without the cost of dependants, i.e. horizontal equity. These took into account the cost of maintaining a family household and supporting dependants through tax exemptions and other allowances, or help in kind. Allowances against income for self and dependants have the effect of reducing the poverty of families, as well as their income inequality compared to other groups. The old principle of the taxable surplus, or ability to pay, demanded that taxation take account not only of the level of income, but also the numbers dependent upon it. Those with dependent children and spouses had a lesser taxable capacity than those without. Also there was a limit, necessary for a reasonable subsistence, below which none should be taxed. If the person is taxed above the 'ability to pay', this will undermine the self-sufficiency of those who might otherwise be able to support themselves and their dependants.

There were also more informal mechanisms – as in the private housing market where mortgage advances were made only on limited multiples of one income. Such paternalistic devices had the effect of holding down prices and making it more likely that borrowers could meet the other costs of running a home. In turn, competition between family members for work, with its downward pull on wage rates, was discouraged through restrictions on child and female labour, and the gender-based wage differentials which were consolidated in the nineteenth century (to replace old guild and trade customs and practice) raised the value of the mother's domestic labour and reduced the opportunity costs of child-rearing.

The increased entry of women into the workforce by the 1970s, plus equal wage and opportunity legislation, followed by positive discrimination, pushed living standards towards a two-income norm. This affected the ability of couples to cooperate effectively to distribute family tasks between them, and made it difficult for fathers to compensate for the loss of a second wage, as the opportunity costs of children rose to make them an expensive use of the mother's time in terms of lost earnings.

Men's jobs had traditionally dominated economies, but the workforce representation of men shrunk enormously and at an accelerating pace due to momentous changes in labour markets. In 1975, 7.5 per cent of males aged 20 to 24 were unemployed, but over 16 per cent by the mid-1980s. Rapid de-industrialization ended massive numbers of jobs in shipbuilding, iron and steel works, motor manufacture, dock work, and other heavy and extractive industries. These had provided generations of working men with a 'living wage', understood as an income sufficient to support a wife and children at a modest standard of comfort. Moreover, the three million relatively well-paid, full-time jobs for semi-skilled or unskilled male factory workers lost between 1960 and 1990 were a major entry point into the world of work for youngsters without the skills or paper qualifications for white-collar work – where, anyway, technology was taking its toll of lower-grade office work.

Labour market and wage developments had their sharpest impact on younger workers. The new de-regularized labour market saw long-term security of tenure often give way to short-term and 'renegotiable' agreements at all levels, in public services, banking and finance, as much as in industry. The rise of the working mother, anxious to keep her employment to a minimum necessary to meet basic commitments, helped companies to 'restructure' with contingent workers. The expansion of part-time work accounted for virtually all the new jobs created in Britain in the 1980s (and, in turn, accounted for the expansion of the female labour force). One result was that the amount of support, if any, that men, especially at younger ages, were able to offer families, was drastically reduced – leading to almost insuperable obstacles to family formation at the bottom of the socio-economic ladder.

The traditional reluctance to threaten the jobs of established workers was based not insignificantly on the rationale that many supported wives and children, but now there were no qualms about the impact on the family. In the 1930s, young men figured lightly among the unemployed. In hard times, family-benefiting measures like child tax allowances were preserved or uprated, even as provisions for other groups, like the elderly, were scaled back to give priority to the nation's families and youth.

Much of the economic restructuring of the Thatcher years was overdue and its aftermath, beneficial. The dark side was its contribution to family disruption and decline. An acceleration in developments so threatening to social cohesion and adequate social reproduction would, in times past, have caused no small consternation and promptly triggered remedial action. The will and the resources would have been marshalled to protect families and children as the social priority group, since they were the repositories of a cherished way of life and the sum of all futures, whose welfare was central to national identity and interests. After the Industrial Revolution, new family-benefiting measures came into being to replace those it had swept away. In the midst of the upheavals of the 1980s, the state could have tried to protect families, but it did not.

Or rather, the pressures on families were furthered by increasingly discriminatory taxation on top of the abandonment of protection in labour and housing markets. In 1978, the Royal Commission on the Distribution of Wealth and Income investigated state transfers and taxes and found that it was fathers who had become the biggest losers, as the tax liabilities of families with children had increased at about four times the rate of those of single people since the 1950s. Afterwards, while most groups saw a reduction in their direct tax burden (the combination of income tax and national insurance), that on families continued to grow – accounting for the paradox of increased taxation during a period of reduced tax rates. At half average income, a family's contribution increased most of all – from 2.4 per cent of income in 1978/9 to 10 per cent by 1995, compared to a drop from 23.5 to 22.3 per cent for a single person. When all taxation is considered, a couple with two children paid only 2 per cent less tax at one and a half average earnings than did a single, childless person by the mid-1990s. Cutting tax rates, while reducing or removing allowances, meant the redistribution of the tax burden to those with family responsibilities from those without children. As national insurance was increasingly relied upon to raise revenue, it fell particularly heavily on parents, as it incorporates no dependant exemptions. Child Benefit, an amalgam of the old Child Tax Allowance and the Family Allowance, which had become the only way of equalizing tax liabilities between those with and those without children, had half the value of the combined tax/Family Allowance of 1960 when it was established. It was under continued threat, being frozen between 1987 and 1990 – before it became the turn of the Married Couple's Tax Allowance to be cut under Major and abolished under Blair.

The dispossession of the family was not inevitable, but a matter of priorities. Whether bad years or good, family-benefiting measures were never 'affordable'. Indeed, they had to be abolished or reduced to fund more deserving causes – whether lower tax bands, increased age-related allowances for the over-65s, higher premiums for income support pensioners, and uprating one-parent benefit faster than the inflation rate. Any help for families had to be paid for by families. They had to pay for the extension of means-tested relief to bail out their own poor, when many would not have fallen below the poverty line if their allowances had not been cut and charges for their dependants imposed in the first place. The movement of income away from families took a fourfold form: away from those with children to individuals without dependants; from one main earner couples to double earner couples; from younger, child-rearing generations to the retired; from two-parent families to lone parents, and joining these in the 1990s, from child-rearing at home to substitute care.

The withdrawal of recognition for the cost of supporting dependants was followed by the imposition of charges for dependants with the Community Charge or poll tax – one of the most anti-family measures anyone could devise. Unrelated to ability to pay or the demand for council services, a flat-rate tax was applied to anyone over 18. Supposedly an individual charge, the responsibility to pay for everyone nonetheless rested upon the household head, so that a couple paid double charges, irrespective of who and how much anyone earned. Again, those pushed below the poverty line could claim a benefit to enable them to pay. The Charge had affinities with feminist proposals to tighten the economic squeeze on families not only by eliminating any marriage allowance, but by taxing husbands for the household services provided by wives to dissuade people from forming couple households.

It is likely that policy-induced changes in incentives interacted with men's unemployment and earnings to disfavour marriage – linking the withdrawal of government support for families with smaller family size, a dramatic rise in single adults, and an increasing incidence of breakdown. When endemic destabilization of male earnings is accompanied by programmes supporting broken families, parenthood outside marriage and serial polygyny become viable options and there is likely to be a shift from one welfare system to another. If the welfare available outside the married state rises enough, any economic reasons for forming a conjugal household disappear. The diminished financial incentives for either parent to marry, or increased incentives to separate, work most at the margins. Men with relatively poor earnings opportunities are competing with the state as providers of resources to mothers of their children and they come out a poor second.

Embarking on such economic transformations as marked the Thatcher years without a family policy spelt disaster on the social front. But did anybody know what a family policy was? They might have thought they did, as they dismissed it as a creature of collectivist interventionists, or a form of misdirected poor relief. It is scarcely credible that those taking office at the end of the 1970s could have been so amnesiac as not to remember that Child Benefit had just taken over from a tax allowance and a family allowance as the only measure of recognition for support of children in the system. But it was constantly condemned as an unjustifiable 'hand-out' and blamed for the rising social security bill, or for being an 'affront' or 'burden' to taxpayers (as if parents were not themselves taxpayers and as if each individual did not have a single, personal tax allowance). Hooray Henriettas told the press how it kept them in gin. Perhaps this was just because it had been called a benefit – yuk! A 'pension' or 'bus pass' or 'tax-cut' attracted no similar odium, even if received by aristocrats or billionaires. Child Benefit represented just over 6 per cent of the social security budget by the mid-1990s, even if, as a previous tax allowance, it should have been treated as revenue forgone. Margaret Thatcher herself favoured children's tax allowances, but made no attempt to switch back. She seems to have regarded the universal benefit as a premium on fecklessness and, like many others, blamed general parental support for the sins of means-tested or 'targeted' welfare – to which the answer was targeted welfare! Otherwise, any remaining acknowledgement of the costs of multiple dependency borne by those above the Income Support line was 'wasted wealth' thrown at 'rich' parents. Never mind that a single person achieved much the same living standard at under a third of the income required for two adults and two adolescents, and a childless couple needed 50 per cent less than a couple with two young children to obtain the same living standard. The more it was diminished, the greater the scapegoat it became and it was more or less accused of bankrupting the state. Its taxation was called for – but this would cost more than it was worth.

If, as elsewhere in the anglophone world, family policy considerations ceased to apply in welfare policy and fiscal strategy, so the remnants and remembrances of family policy measures became a source of puzzlement, as to why these should ever have existed. Welfare states in which family policy was, in part, embedded, were subjected to scrutiny in terms of vertical equity objectives, or as if egalitarianism was their primary purpose. It was mused that maybe such measures were misplaced or misapplied public assistance, or a muddled, inadequate means to redistribute wealth, leading to both left and right getting lathered up about resources not being 'targeted on the poor' or given instead to those not in 'need'. Socialists objected that the welfare state did not redistribute income and wealth as they had hoped, and was little more than a smokescreen to disguise the failings and contradictions of capitalism. Now they were joined by conservatives, claiming that the middle classes were benefiting more than the 'poor', by making use of health services, education and tax breaks. If the system did not do 'what it is designed to do' – make sure only those in 'need' receive a benefit – then it must have got waylaid or misappropriated. All was quite time blind, so ignorant and ignoring of history.

It is unlikely that Collectivist or Christian demands to equalize the life chances of those who did badly out of the market's allocation, by passing resources from rich to poor, ever had much appeal. For most people, 'the Robin Hood approach to sharing income held few promises and many threats if pressed too far. Their hopes for personal betterment would be thwarted if opportunities to get ahead were closed, or if others came to think of them as rich and hence to be penalized.' More attractive was the welfare state as a type of personal insurance which safeguards the individual against risks or misfortunes which threaten living standards. This functions like a national insurance company. As, over a lifetime, the individual's needs vary enormously, so resources move from one of the phases to another, smoothing out the peaks and troughs. Those who have few resources at any stage in life could be given assistance drawn from the pooled resources of those richer than themselves. But for the majority the welfare state would mainly help move resources across time, temporarily rather than permanently, as individuals went through life.

Even so, it is doubtful if many family protection measures should come under the rubric of 'the welfare state' – however defined. Family protection measures were something distinct which were incorporated into fiscal and welfare systems, industrial and commercial organizations, professional and private insurance systems and government strategies, in different ways at different times. And, while child-rearing was a heavily burdened phase of life, which might push many into poverty, the impetus for giving parents support often went beyond any income maintenance or insurance principle. Beveridge emphasized that a coherent family policy was essential to the growth of prosperity and abolition of want, as a means of 'maintaining individual freedom and responsibilities, and the family as the unit of the state', without undermining the liberal, capitalist order. Health and education provision involved investments in further generations necessary for the perpetuation of society and the public good, as well as personal well-being. In turn, family allowances were favoured in that they had labour market objectives, in not having the disincentive effects of selective poor relief on the work of family providers. They alleviated financial stress while maintaining work incentives, or 'kept the floor of wages above the ceiling of benefits'. Given that they also removed pressure on the general wage rate by fathers of families, or made possible equal wages without threatening the breadwinner's children, they frequently antedate welfare states and were often paid on a firm or industry basis, or by local authorities, as well as trade and professional associations (on the insurance basis), in continental Europe, the USA and Australia (where the earliest payments were made to fathers from a levy in the Commonwealth Public Service in 1920).

The social consequences of a means-tested welfare system based on meeting 'need' are appalling and should have been known to anyone with a shred of historical knowledge. However, if you are time blind, enthusiastic and gullible, nothing looks so immediately attractive, so seemingly cheap and efficient as 'targeting' the 'needy' and the 'casualties'. While the advent of 'targeting' might have seemed a return to a nineteenth-century concept of a more limited role for the state in welfare to both friends and enemies, this overlooks the way in which considerations of family protection would have applied even then (as in industry, where wages were subjected to forces other than those of the market). The trouble is, the 'needy' are not a finite group, neatly separated off from the great majority of 'well off' families. The range of family income is not that wide. Help restricted to the poor simply means more poor people. Inside means-testing's web of disincentives, welfare erodes the work ethic, honesty, family structure and social norms. What incentive is there to work if you lose benefits, incur expenses and pay so much tax that you are hardly any better off? What incentive is there to raise earnings when you are only a few pence better off? Why double up, cooperate and collaborate, when means-tested benefits will give as much or more to you for going solo?

A perennial temptation to solve the disincentives problems created by 'targeting' is to be less selective. So, disregard more income for benefit purposes, or give extra 'top ups'. As the ball rolls on, a measure to deal with disincentives at one point in the system creates or exacerbates disincentives at another, so there is a further 'benefit to get off of benefit'. If top ups are given for part-time work to make people work at all, and they stick here, then another benefit is in order to work full time. There is con-stant pressure on the system to let more people in as, at the same time, those on the margins change their behaviour to qualify or stay eligible. So many poor people. So little to meet all the 'need'? Cut general reliefs for parents, the simple-minded solution dictates; make the 'rich' pay – for is it not self-evident that all these poor people exist because others get help they do not 'need'? As general help for families is reduced further, the poverty and unemployment traps worsen, since the rate of earnings over which people are subject to high taxation and benefit withdrawal widen. It is impossible to 'help the poor' without trapping them, if those above them are being pulled down at the same time, so that the needies are as well or better off than the 'rich'. No wonder Income Support for working-age people and Housing Benefit were up fivefold and top ups for working poor families were up twentyfold in constant prices from 1979 to the mid-1990s.

What a mess. Keith Joseph regretted, with hindsight, the intro-duction of Family Income Supplement in the early 1970s to deal with the growing problem of poor, working families. It was poor economics not to have uprated the child tax allowance or Family Allowance instead, particularly since the problem had much of its origin in the erosion of general help for child-rearing – which removes far more people from poverty than 'targeting the needy' ever did or will. Frank Field, ex-director of the Child Poverty Action Group agrees. He had once campaigned on the platform of increasing the Family Allowance while 'clawing' this back from 'rich' parents by reducing their tax allowance. The Minister at the time had to explain that, carried to its conclusion, it would mean fathers of several children leaving the factory gate with a negative wage packet.

While, at first glance, means-tested and selective benefits are eminently appealing – not least because 'cost saving' translates as immediate savings to welfare budgets – no attention is paid to the dynamic consequences, or to the behavioural change which makes the historical record so awful. On its own terms, it fails. After all, between 1979 and 1990 mean and median annualized income grew by 2.9 and 2.1 per cent respectively, but the poorest quintile group gained 0.4 per cent, compared to 3.8 per cent in the richest group.

If Charles Murray is identified as the demon instructing the Thatcherite Tories, then they could not have read him very closely. Murray linked the upsurge in drop-out from the labour force, welfare dependency, family dissolution and illegitimacy – that 'demographic wonder, without precedent in the American experience' – with the way in which the numbers of the US poor stopped shrinking in the early 1970s and began to grow. Welfare for lone mothers discouraged providers from remaining as the family support, and its availability militated against the formation of the family in the first place. The result is the circular process: men do not strive to be good providers and women do not expect it or put pressure on men to behave responsibly. A licence to earn while on welfare is not just an incentive to work. It provides 'a much stronger incentive for women who were not on welfare to get on it and then become trapped in it'. The net effect is to raise the value of being eligible for welfare and thereby, 'via a classic market response, increase the supply of eligible women', as people in female-headed families were a growing proportion of the non-aged poor, more likely to be persistently poor, and the children of welfare-dependent mothers were more likely to become welfare dependent themselves. Such was targeting. Bizarrely, its malign effects were attributed to the (now threadbare) remains of general family contingent support!

So crude was the understanding that clumsy attempts to deal with the issues involved ignominiously backfired. Peter Lilley could not see the difference between saying that women have children just to obtain benefits such as housing and accepting that, by socializing the costs of child-rearing, the welfare state has made the rapid growth of lone-parent families and unstable partnering feasible and acceptable – so he waved his 'little list' of benefit cheats like 'young ladies who get pregnant just to jump the housing list'. How it did it is one thing. But how could the Party of the family abandon the family to its burden and fate? Has it not been Conservatives who stressed the maintenance of institutions, for is it not as great a conceit for individuals to believe that they can cobble up their own lives, or reinvent the world every minute, as for the ideologue to believe that he can mould society in his own image?

Institutions stand for the unity and continuity of the community and its creative wisdom, where 'in the institutions of the nation . . . there appears a fundamental unity beyond the ken of individual reasoning, a unity of national purpose', so the 'maintenance of institutions' was customarily defined as 'a sacred duty of Conservatism'. Was not the 'family' precisely a morally loaded concept embodying an ideal image, or model of relationships and obligations, to be striven for and supported irrespective of the numbers or living arrangements approximating to it? Cannot Conservatism be characterized as arising from a sense of belonging to some continuing and pre-existing social order, a covenant between the dead, the living and the unborn? Linking these, the family is surely – as an end in itself and a means to all the rest – the clearest example of an institution based upon a transcendental bond and as the 'first community' or initial principle, model and guarantee of a stable, consensual society? It is the primary moral domain: the place where the moral enterprise first gets under way, and is at its most lucid. It is the focus of fundamental ethical concerns, whether with the fate of the world beyond our lifetime, the transmission of accumulated wisdom or concern for the welfare of others. It is the key link in the social chain, mediating between the individual and other institutions.

Therefore, is it not the responsibility of government – and what it once meant to be the party of the family – to maintain the arrangements in which freedom can be pursued and preserved and individual abilities can flower? Is it not to ensure continuity with cohesion – not minister to their ruin in the dust of atoms? And, if the goal is to strengthen, not assume, the functions of families, does it not mean affirming that intact families are good, and that parents who spent time and resources to create and raise children are demonstrably doing a good thing by those children, and for society as a whole?

Defenders of liberal capitalism have recognized how family values are both at odds with competitive individualism, yet essential if the egocentricity, autonomy and acquisitiveness at its heart are not to plunge it into anarchy and abuse and shred social life itself. There is something paradoxical about the juxtaposition of a naked self-interest that presumably motivates efficient allocation of market resources and the altruism that purportedly motivated the allocation of resources within the family. Milton Friedman observed that 'liberals . . . take freedom of the individual, or perhaps the family, as our ultimate goal in judging social arrangements', when this comprised 'one of the most profound contradictions in liberal social theory'. Individuals as intentional actors pursue strategies towards the achievement of their chosen ends *vis-à-vis* the state and in the consumption sphere of the economy. But in the political arena and in the marketplace, father and mother putatively make choices that represent a balanced aggregation of the wants and needs of family members. Family obligations are owed simply in recognition of ties which are at the opposite pole to transactions or relationships based on principles of contract or exchange, which might reasonably be wound up if the profits fail to materialize. The self-sacrifice and care shown in parental behaviour appear as moral imperatives involving binding mutual interdependence and willingness to forgo self-gratification and gain for the sake of others. To treat them as such will wreck the family, just as self-actualization and self-gratification, unrestrained by commitment, threatens the world with egotism and aggression. Where wealth and status are closely associated, parental responsibilities have always been in danger of being downgraded through the costs and loss of competitiveness which they impose. Then, if families come to have lower living standards or are more impoverished compared to those without dependants, both may come to believe that there is little or no value placed on raising children, or caring for others. Family life will seem a worthless and wasteful impediment to individual consumption and accumulation. It was family values which provided an impetus for those compensatory measures which, in reducing the standard-of-living penalty and the opportunity costs of child-rearing, upheld its esteem. In turn, the moral basis of the state's intervention in marriage lay in a commitment to family stability for socially constructive ends, by confirming lifelong monogamous unions. If it was crucial to preserve the marriage bond from self-interest, then everywhere law intertwined with obligation to stress the altruistic components in family relations.

In the general counter-cultural estrangement and revolt against the legacy of Western civilization which erupted in the 1960s, institutions became the trenches of the opposition to be taken or destroyed. A nihilistic concept of freedom developed alongside a belief that people were merely the products of processes or social forces and that their behaviour mindlessly mirrored their circumstances. Ties of mutual obligation appeared useless and opposed to freedom, and the family became the chief instrument of a pernicious process of conditioning, which enslaved individuals with all their potential for free fulfilment. Freedom was now pursued in opposition to social relations, because the promise was that a managerial state could ensure social harmony or bring about 'spontaneous consensus' by getting the controlling conditions right. Create a good environment, meet all needs, and all products will be satisfactory, even perfect.

At the time Margaret Thatcher took office, there was widespread disillusionment with the pretensions of expert, progressive elites, who supposedly were able to direct human affairs from their knowledge of the determining conditions. Unfortunately, this failed to result in the rediscovery and reassertion of social life as a moral order. The great tragedy of the Thatcher years is that Conservatism did not reoccupy the ground between the unreal polarities of the collective will and the individual. It had to be said – there is no such thing as 'society'. Human action is not controlled by determining forces, which render free will and choice illusory. There is no supra being 'society', no entity or personality whose existence is externally and concretely embodied in tangible goods of its own. There is no historical necessity or will to divine, no 'society' or 'system' to speak for, appeal to, or put in the dock.

On the face of it, this appeared to reconnect with nineteenth-century liberalism. This denied the existence of any will beyond the individual wills of the members of society, and of any common good beyond concern with general as against sectional interests. While the sum of existent thought is more than can ever inhabit the mind of any individual, this does not mean that there is a unitary social mind, or a separate autonomous entity. It only refers to the mass of communicable ideas operative in any society. T. H. Green and L. T. Hobhouse stressed that while rights could only be interpreted within the context of social life, it was a condition of free development of the individual as a moral being that he was an end in himself. The state could and must be used to sustain the basis of common life, but its ends or objectives had to be the same as those of individuals.

Notions of society as an organism are as old as political thought and were usually used to emphasize the mutual dependence between the members of a society. However, once 'society' or the 'people' or a process was vested with its own consciousness and purposes, this justified an interventionist theory of the state. While liberalism had decreed the state to be used only for human, ethical ends, increases in state power were the concomitant of the transformation of this means into an end. This undermined the old democratic idea that every member had the same share of power in determining social actions and even that each man's life was of equal value. The individual, subordinated to the state or the social organism need not necessarily share or even comprehend the purpose to which he might be put – with the kind of consequences seen in Nazi Germany and the Communist states. With the expert as opposed to the responsible ruler necessary to formulate policies based on a knowledge of society's will or 'needs' this, as Herbert Spencer had sourly observed, meant domination by unaccountable cliques squandering communal resources as they furthered their own interests and ideological proclivities.

Nothing in old liberalism obviated the way that human understanding resides in, is acquired, and modified, only through social experience. The individual is responsible for his choices, but it hardly follows that he forms out of nothing, owes nothing to anyone, and is the origin of meaning and sensibility. But its modern successors came to believe that freedom might reside in the sheer fact of choice, not upon the types of choices we make in terms of important aims and values. In turn, the notion of choice was applied to all the institutions in which the individual had his being, and without which there would hardly be choices to make. Neo-liberalism, committed to notions of the impartiality of markets, and the person as a rational utility-maximizing, self-oriented being, called into question any and all collective structures that could serve as an impediment to the logic of the pure market – including the nation, work groups, unions, associations, co-operatives and the family. This was somewhat perverse for, at the time, the rediscovery of institutions was proceeding apace in economics and it was increasingly appreciated that institutions determined rules and that rules structured incentives. But, in politics, the market moved from an unsurpassed means to ends, like prosperity, to become not only an end in itself, whose imperatives admitted of nothing but submission, but an authority telling us there were no values to embody in public policy. Whatever the market dictated was right and right was whatever the market dictated. There was implicit, if not outright, denial that values arose from other considerations and bases than markets (which represented the results of countless actions in certain defined relations) or that values might in any way affect the social life in which markets operate and hence determine what should or should not be regarded as commodities. '"Trust Evolution" said the extreme Socialist and the extreme Individualist' in H. G. Wells' *Things to Come*, 'as piously as the Christians put their trust in God'. In 1980, for evolution, read market.

This not only removed any grounds for ring-fencing or protecting the family against market pressures – and at a time when it was under unprecedented attack. It also affirmed it as just one form of self-expression with no communal basis or worth. The state could do nothing but stand aside as the people made their 'choices', or do nothing beyond offering humanitarian relief to any 'casualties'. The world was now one of autonomous and self-regarding individuals with random living arrangements and sensory experiences disconnected from each other, the future and the past – flies of the summer who might associate, if at all, for passing convenience. Children were not significant in terms of the continuance of any identity, be it national, cultural, familial, and useless to anybody or anything beyond their progenitors' indulgence. This empty solipsism was mono-generational. Parenting was an 'expensive hobby', or an otherwise meaningless activity or personal eccentricity and, as such, a drain upon the maximization of the discretionary time and resources which enable us to live for ourselves alone.

Taxes on mutual support, like the Community Charge, vindicated the isolated self-serving existence. To justify it, families were castigated as a burden on others and for occupying too much of the world, compared with the solitary person or the 'little widow' or the 'lone parent', who was the virtuous entirety of a seemingly self-contained, costless existence. But human beings are hardly designed to live alone. Sooner or later they need help, and this has to come from other people – even if the fiction of independence is maintained by costly armies of helpers. Atomized people do not use fewer resources, they use more. Atomized people do not need less support, but more, or have fewer problems, or occupy less space, but more. There was an avoidance of all questions about the circumstances in which people provided for each other, as distinct from those which fostered reliance on public provisions of all kinds. There was no appreciation that the bulk of welfare and order, and the efficient use of resources, come from the family, and thus no inkling that family stability might be a public good.

Everywhere, with crime, civil disorder, environmental pressures, health, housing, there were problems related to the loosening and breaking of relationships – which stood to be exacerbated by bonuses on fragmentation. The tendency for more people to live alone made it less likely that they could deal with their own and their relatives' crises, as much as it put pressure on land use. An increase in one-adult households meant more children at risk of poor care (who would contribute to young homelessness), and so more demand for social services and institutional provision. Ministers insisted that crime and violence were matters of values and that a revival of moral constraints was essential to halt their inexorable climb. But there was that inability to progress to the second stage and understand that shared values and restraints were not acquired as a one-off lesson, but were part of a way of life. The individual bereft of social ties has great difficulty acquiring moral assurance in childhood and great difficulty retaining it as an adult. If the number of unattached individuals in the community is a good predictor of crime, then family disintegration encouraged this, within the household and through the loosening network of family control and participation in the community. Society required that immediate authority of allegiance that transcended contract and countered self-interest. It is an increasing and ineffectual struggle to maintain order if the individual has to do a cost–benefit analysis before deciding whether or not to obey any particular regulation. This will not be forthcoming where the principles of loyalty, service and mutuality – as might be embodied in the family and extended into other institutions – command no respect and are inoperative. Individualism will undermine the civil order as this expresses itself independently of the institutions in which individual development advances in tune with the common good, and the constraints which are its precondition. In deconstructing the very institutions required for a minimal state, and in leaving a moral void and social vacuum, neo-liberals must perforce call on the state to adopt roles civil society would previously have performed.

There can be no morally neutral tax/benefit system. Each will reward some kinds of behaviour and penalize others. They also promote certain assumptions and values. As seen with the Community Charge debates then, and now, support for a flat-rate, individual charge is invariably accompanied by rabid expressions of hatred for children and for family life as an intolerable imposition on single, childless, people. A tax structure oblivious to dependencies itself suggests that raising children is just another act of consumption, and their status little different from that of a dog or a car. Double tax for couples or exemptions for single people are a consumption tax on earning spouses, equivalent to a television or road licence. This is the fiscal equivalent of the way in which family life is publicly relegated to just a matter of taste or personal inclination in a world of competing 'sexualities'. Where everybody has his or her own definition of family life and the individual chooses what is and is not a family – which can always be redefined, reconstructed and discarded; there are none to protect.

Clearly, values influence tax, benefit and other policies as well as flow from them. Suggestions that family trends owe a great deal to the actions of policy-makers – whether or not the outcomes were intended – are contrary to the persistent dogma that government is incapable of influencing developments in this field. Many of those who gave pride of place to the role of economics in behaviour were among the first to deny that material considerations made any difference to family and marital decisions. The belief that family trends cannot be explained in economic terms shades into the belief that these are beyond understanding – yet there is no reason why they are any more unintelligible or beyond human influence than other social or physical phenomena.

Even more remarkable perhaps has been the idea that nothing untoward is happening. There is evolution, not dissolution. Family and household structures have just become more 'diverse', with people living in a greater 'variety' of structures than ever before. With the definition of family stretched to cover virtually any living situation and all transitional states, these multifarious 'new family forms' are simply personal choices, or inventions, or lifestyle decisions where what people want, people unerringly get. And, if these originate simply as personal creations then, truly, the state is powerless when it comes to family trends. Those hostile to the nuclear family have eagerly turned projections of its virtual demise in the near future into prophecies which we are obliged to help achieve. Its friends or, anyway, those who have no particular brief to do it ill, have taken consolation and refuge from a contentious, painful subject in the same determinism. It has also been dangerous territory. Sir Keith Joseph's 'pills for proles' speech in October 1974 ended his chances of succeeding Edward Heath as leader of the Conservative Party by suggesting that the lowest social classes be given every assistance to stop reproducing.

Furthermore, to even try to help might do untold harm. Do not intervene: as if a million and one laws and regulations, everyday actions, environmental conditions and constraints – from laws forbidding the selling or drowning of babies, to the price of shoes – were not interventions, influences and intrusions. Indeed, claims that government was completely powerless in the face of family trends and that these changes taking place were desirable, inevitable and irreversible have been about as hollow as similar claims about British industry in the 1970s. Interestingly, none of this precluded taking from families to help families. As Daniel Patrick Moynihan observed, it virtually obliged you to take away anything and everything that had sustained them for generations.

All was underwritten by Ferdinand Mount's *The Subversive Family* – arriving just at the right time to tell politicians that the best thing to do was nothing. The family, Mount declared, was something outside of social systems, and it did not need help. Those who meddled in this area had its worst interests at heart. At the same time, it could survive anything. This was a green light for plunder. The surviving measures of family support provided a reservoir of funds through which the expansion of welfare was paid for by the primary welfare institution.

The loss of basic guiding principles about the value of family life at policy-making level encouraged the occupation of this field by sectional interests, with an increasing tendency to give special treatment to those who were well organized and active in pursuing a narrow set of interests. The rise of lone parents and their disproportionate reliance on expanding means-tested and selective benefits meant that what would be, anyway, an active pressure group, was mobilized by women's rights and feminist interests. The increases in lone parents, pensioners and disability claimants suggest that the pressure on resources involved makes their situation unfavourable compared to intact families, the young and healthy since their cost to the state is so much greater. Exactly the opposite occurred, because public decisions have been increasingly influenced by the power of interest groups and power is partly a function of size. The larger the role of transfers going to growing groups and the bigger the role of government in guaranteeing and, the more advantageous it is to be in an expanding dependency group. A multiplier effect exists: support increases numbers, while the supply of, for example, intact families, falls as resources are transferred away. The more the state accommodates a client group, the less it feels able to refuse and the more fearful it is of creating offence. No such group ever represents itself as anything but poverty stricken, maligned, discriminated against and generally put upon. It also pays to be exquisitely sensitive to anything that can be construed as insulting, critical or uncaring, and to put on the most extravagant display of outrage, as this leads to compensatory or propitiatory awards.

As might have been predicted, more and more fathers declined to pay for their children. By the end of the 1980s only 30 per cent of lone parents were receiving regular maintenance. Decreasing maintenance accompanied the increasingly casual nature of relationships, with divorced mothers the most likely to receive maintenance (40 per cent in 1989), and never-married mothers the least (14 per cent), and then at very low levels. Never-married mothers were less likely to know who or where the father was, and to want maintenance. The 1991 Child Support Act was an attempt to close the stable door. The essence of the change was a move from a legal system dealing with child maintenance on a case by case, discretionary basis to an administrative system which assessed all maintenance according to the same criteria. If an aim was that of achieving a high level of maintenance, especially from the absentee fathers of lone-parent children on welfare, this has meant little more than a statement of intent. Little consideration was given to the ability of many of the absent men to pay much at all, and how much any savings in this direction counterbalanced the costs of the immense bureaucracy necessary to assess and collect it. The appeasement of interest groups added to the complexities and difficulties of collection. Effectively, no penalties were imposed for non-compliance, the sums involved have been continually whittled down, and the circumstances of appeal seemingly endlessly extended. Lone parents could evade ever naming the man in the first place by pleading a perceived threat to their personal safety. Men's groups waved the shrouds of those who had, purportedly, taken their lives when faced with a demand for child support from a heartless machinery depriving endearing, ousted daddies of 'every penny they have got' and preventing them finding happiness in a second, third, or subsequent, family.

Novel methods of child-rearing would be impossible without substantial support from taxpayers and, as predicted, the Child Support Act has proven to be a blip on a curve showing a progressive rise in the socialization of the costs of child-rearing.

The emergence of AIDS as a major public health issue in the 1980s, and the hijacking of health education to promote gay issues, 'represents an extreme example of the way in which the concerns of minority groups (known as rent-seekers) can demand and obtain disproportionate allocations of public resources by the use of political pressure'. As the government began to squander a fortune on a peril that did not exist, it became the hapless conduit for the triumph of the counter-culture in the full flowering of the sexual revolution.

When AIDS made its appearance in the early 1980s – far more than a major public health problem, it was treated as an epidemic which could reach the level of a national catastrophe. Claims were that soon 'almost every family will be affected by the AIDS problem in some way . . . well over 1,000 British women are carrying the AIDS virus . . . it will go on in a terrible human chain . . . the number of AIDS cases in Britain is really rocketing . . .'. As tens of thousands of people died, 'Society might collapse under the weight of so many deaths of productive people, or the cost of their medical care.' Initially, this appeared to make those claims about sex being virtually the only activity, unlike drugs, drink and tobacco, which was perfectly harmless, no matter how often indulged, seem somewhat hollow. Everything had a price after all – even the directive 'if it feels good, do it'. At the very least, observers feared, we would see a renewed emphasis on monogamy and sexual fidelity. At worst, if we were not careful, there might be persecution of those with free sexual habits. Indeed, 'a dark but predictable side of human nature is that any mysterious epidemic will give rise to scapegoating.'

It is difficult to overestimate the importance, attention and money allocated for HIV/AIDS. As commented in a ten-year overview, the public policy response was 'unusual if not exceptional': the funding was earmarked and no other area of medicine received such high levels of resources. Regional Health Authorities (RHAs) spent tens of times more on each patient with AIDS and thousands of time more on each AIDS death than on, for example, those with heart disease. Yet, and 'at a time of financial stringency in the public services and especially when many claim that the NHS is underfunded', the majority of RHAs underspent their AIDS budgets, while ring-fencing stopped surpluses being reallocated. This involved very large sums; despite all the attempts to get rid of the money through 'schemes inviting ridicule'. This did not prevent the RHAs' budget being increased from £127.5 million in 1990/91 to £137.3 million in 1991/2 and to £181.5 million in 1993/4. HIV/AIDS provided levels of employment unprecedented in medical history, with about as many full-time workers as people with the disease – not including those employed by local authorities, charities, research councils and industry. The HIV/AIDS sector of public employment had a: 'mind boggling proliferation of "jobs" such as Safe Sex advisers, condom project workers, HIV liaison workers, Aids ethnic outreach workers, local Aids health coordinators. Prefix "Aids" or "HIV" to "coordinator", "liaison officer", "worker" and link this to an area of welfare provision such as children, teenagers, women, IUDS, ethnic minorities, prisons, the deaf, disabled, etc., and you have a £17,000–£20,000 job. The big growth this year [1991/2] is Safe Sex education in schools, where the bureaucracy want to provide for kids as young as eight years old.'

Many full-time personnel had no professional qualifications and were often employed by organizations not subject to formal audit. Adding up the helplines, counselling services, information networks, HIV units and so forth, gave about one AIDS organization for every three sufferers. Ironically, the abolition of the Greater London Council and spending constraints on local authorities by the late 1980s intended, not least, to rein in the far left, allowed activists to board the AIDS gravy train by migrating to the centrally funded 'voluntary' sector. Under the pretext of health education, central government was empowering sexual revolutionaries more effectively and without any of the fuss that went with similar moves by the local left.

While it was estimated in 1987 that deaths and new infections would be running at 100,000 a year by the mid-1990s, the figure was reduced to 30,000 the following year and down to 13,000 in

1990 and to 6,000 in 1991. The total number of people who died from the disease after it first appeared and up to mid-1994 was 6,388. A further 3,058 had the disease. In this same period, 2,500,000 had died of cardiovascular diseases, and 60,000 on the roads, including a great many children. Moreover, the death figures were likely to have been inflated by diseases which can accompany, but are not necessarily caused by, the HIV virus and occur in its absence. While an educational campaign assumed 'that all of the sexually active population and infants of all mothers are potentially or actually at risk', AIDS offered virtually no threat to women and children. In the whole decade from 1981 to 1991, there were only nine deaths of women not in an obviously high-risk category. The inaccuracy of the forecasts was no obstacle to a continued misuse of public funds, since extraordinarily generous expenditure has been in the interests of the service producers and pressure groups. As the disease became fashionable, the AIDS establishment consolidated – helped along by the attentions of media, politicians, royalty and celebrities.

Despite the doomsday scenario, in no sense was there an AIDS epidemic in the UK or any developed country – or was there likely to be one. This should have been obvious form the start. Here was a blood–borne infection that was difficult to acquire, unless it was injected into the blood stream – by anal intercourse or syringes. The government's health advisers must have known that blood-borne infections (like hepatitis B) are difficult to transmit and self-limiting in clearly identifiable groups. At the same time, they also ought to have known about the parallel rise in rectal gonorrhoea in men, and put both in the context of the burgeoning 'gay scene'. Over three-quarters of deaths involved men engaged in what gay activists termed 'fast lane sex'. The risk to anyone outside high-risk groups like promiscuous homosexuals, bisexuals and intravenous drug users from the HIV virus was 'negligible'. If an epidemic theory was correct, it may have made sense to spend on general education, as when the population is instructed in personal hygiene to prevent the spread of infection. However, when evidence suggests instead that the primary factors are behavioural, not infectious, then action on the basis of 'externalities' is invalid. Given the determinants of the original and continuing incidence, health education should have been directed at specific groups and concentrated upon desistence from high-risk behaviour, in a similar approach to that used with smoking. The disease could have been stopped in its tracks.

But anything which treated the causal sexual practices like smoking was unthinkable. As it was even claimed that 'gay men' were sacrificing themselves to warn the rest of us, this would deny AIDS victims any symbolic status or significant or heroic role. Homosexual activists wanted both a cure for AIDS at any price and the full legitimization of their lifestyle, and from the beginning the government was guided by the homosexual lobby. The fact that certain sexual practices spread the disease was something that many refused to contemplate, so they tried to protect themselves, and homosexuals, from this knowledge. Anyone trying to be specific about the mode of infection would be accused of being insensitive and hateful, or suffering from 'homophobia'. Instead, the appearance of HIV/AIDS became the platform for the promotion of the chief activity associated with it and of homosexuality as a completely valid, if not superior, lifestyle. The media put itself in the forefront of a propaganda mission, with both specialized services for homosexuals and general promulgation of positive images of homosexuality. The pretext that AIDS 'does not discriminate' and that 'gay or straight' everyone was at risk, provided access to the population at large and to schoolchildren. HIV/AIDS education meant that children had never been exposed to so much sex, from so many directions, so young – both directly in the schools and, indirectly, from its effect on the world around them. What had once been obscure sexual practices scarcely known to old sailors, let alone your mother, were now on the lips of young children. To emphasize the seriousness of the disease denied any quarter to personal and moral sensibilities. The price was life and, in the words of the British Government's initial campaign, people might 'Die of Ignorance'.

With a green light, all and any lewdness could now high-mindedly parade as 'health' information, whose disseminators were performing a public duty, whether in the woman's magazine or sex education lesson. We now lived in Pornopolis. Advertisements, television, magazines, now displayed and discoursed on the details of all kinds of permutations of sexual activities. The full acceptance of homosexual practice as a model for all relationships was central to the 'sexual revolution' – a pivotal role for homosexuality which also made AIDS victims martyrs for love, or sacrificial victims of an oppressive society. The radical objectives of the 1960s counterculture eruption went beyond the ending of discrimination against minority sexual preferences as a drive against all categorization and regulation. Inhabiting a world without gender, people would couple and uncouple in 'partnerships' unconscious of each other's biological sex membership, free from the bondage of ancient prejudice in a golden time of universal emancipation. If nothing else, 'alternative sex' symbolized the unbounded ego and became a challenge to anything that was in the way. As the family was the foremost institution against which the individual must assert himself, it stood accused of creating the categories of male and female and 'constructing' the strait-jacket of heterosexuality itself. Homosexuals acquired tremendous significance in being unburdened by exclusive attachments or family commitments, and in epitomizing sex without constraint. The counter-culture insistence that the individual be 'the centre of my own world' was mirrored in the self-absorbed hedonism and narcissism of homosexuality – in opposition to 'the one institution that has served mankind since the dawn of history . . . the basic cell upon which every known civilization has been built'. Homosexuality is the ultimate challenge and final solution to the family. The pivotal role of homosexuality in the sexual revolution also made AIDS victims martyrs for love, or sacrificial victims of an oppressive society.

Homosexual lobbies were incensed by Section 46 of the 1986

Education Act and the 'notorious' clause 28 of the Local Government Act 1988. These were the results of parents' and private members' attempts to restrain the aggressive promotion of homosexuality from nursery to higher education by left-wing local authorities in their 'positive images' campaigns of the 1980s. The 1986 Education Act required that school governors ensure that sex education 'is given in such a manner as to encourage those pupils to have due regard to moral considerations and the value of family life'. Parents were also granted the statutory right to appeal when unhappy about the lessons, although governors had discretion over how to respond. Section 28 of the 1988 Local Government Act prohibited local authorities from 'intentionally promoting homosexuality or publishing material with that intention and from promoting the teaching in any maintained school of homosexuality as a pretended family relationship'. Neither of these were the Government measures that critics have lambasted as the apogee of Thatcherite repression – even if it might be claimed that, by not killing the amendments, the government had 'given way to the moral right' (Giles Radice, Labour's Education spokesman). 'We must all', Ian McKellen told an anti-clause rally 'be out and about, in the streets, in the classrooms . . . promoting homosexuality.' Maybe the Government had some small regard for those other than the homosexual lobby. John Major endeavoured to make it up to McKellen and placate militant homosexual groups like Stonewall by leap-frogging the offending legislation and using the National Curriculum as AIDS education for 11- to 14-year-olds was made a compulsory part of the Science course. Dropped as the curriculum overloaded, it reappeared, of course, as a requirement in sex education, albeit with the proviso that parents could withdraw children.

Rather than that this presided over a repressive imposition of high Victorian values, it is truer to say that Thatcher–Major Governments were 'unable to reverse a single part of the cultural revolution, not least because it barely tried, and did not understand it'. Yet, ironically, both the Thatcher and Major administrations were brought down by the subversive family. The Community Charge spelt the end of Thatcher's premiership. The cutting of the marriage allowance by Major's Chancellor Kenneth Clarke – as he condemned it as an 'anomaly' – threw away the only card that, in the last analysis, would return the Tories to power. Abolition of the marriage allowance threatened a big tax rise for millions; a threat that would always keep Labour out of power – until the Tories did the dirty themselves.

Notes

1   The 'cause' of child prostitution is said to be Thatcherism, a 'product of the housing and social security policies of the 1980s and the radical redistribution of wealth in favour of the prosperous . . .' A commentary blames heterosexual 'society, families, schools and the law' for denying gay children 'rites of passage enjoyed by their heterosexual peers . . .', again it seems due to Thatcherism. Homeless children and young people are an aspect of a 'dramatic growth in childhood poverty', which began in the 1980s – with Thatcher. They are right-on little revolutionaries 'taking to the streets' in protest at 'neo-conservative policies which reduced the capacity of the social security system, voluntary and statutory social service agencies, and the education and youth services, to respond to those children when they found themselves in difficulties'. A wider tale speaks of how Britain has always been marked by inequalities of class, whether in terms of wealth and income, health and educational opportunity, 'or any other feature of social life'. Inequalities began to narrow due to 'the growing resistance and refusal on the part of the working-class people to accept both their unequal lot in life and the naked operation of a market system that produced and reproduced this', and the fears of the rich. Cautious and gradual social reforms culminated in 'a so-called "welfare state" between 1949 and the mid-1970s', to modify the 'most brutal consequences of a market economy'. Disaster struck and: 'the governments of Margaret Thatcher brought an abrupt end to the achievements of the welfare state'. Recessions, 'spurred on by government policy, saw mass unemployment return and poverty increase dramatically', as the bosses clawed 'back what power they had lost'. The 'rise in theft and burglary occurred in the Thatcher years, when there was no such thing as society, unemployment rates were high, and the gap between the rich and the poor grew dramatically'; 'the illegality of drugs puts them into the hands of organized crime . . . and . . . forces addicts to commit muggings in their desperation for money'. If 'heroin and cocaine be sold . . . in safe quality and quantity in Boots . . . crime would vanish at a stroke'. (Available evidence on relationships between unemployment and the growth of crime in the UK, shows virtually no connection, and even an

obverse one in the period 1971–91. Anyway, crime was well into the ascendancy by the 1960s.)

2   Not that Britain was all alone in this. Australia, for example, saw an enormous upsurge in the numbers dependent upon supporting parent benefit, and a subsequent rapid rate of increase, after the six-months qualifying period was removed in 1980. (The numbers rose fivefold in ten years.) By 1991–92 the federal government was providing about ten times as much support to children of separated parents as to children in intact families.

7 Government control of school education

Dennis O'Keeffe

In British arrangements for mass education today, the main participants or stakeholders – parents, teachers, pupils, students – are not
able adequately to communicate or express or give effect to their
preferences, and so end up being practically powerless to affect
policy. Politicians and educational bureaucrats, not operating with
their own private financial resources, make policy. Public finance
and public provision of education affect curriculum, pedagogy and
evaluation.[1] The results are that given material is less well taught,
and dubious educational practices arise.

The Thatcher Era may have seen remarkable achievements for
British society, especially with improvements on the economic
front. However, it maintained the deleterious effects of a very
inadequate education system, one increasingly less vigorous in
the clear-sighted pursuit of knowledge and virtue, and this is
maintained to this day. Why did British schools and colleges not
improve commensurately with the commercial economy? After
all, human capital, the output of the educational system, is crucial
to modern economic life. While British society was brought face
to face with the demands of modernity – with the imperatives of
competition and clear rights of property – the task of doing the
same to education was left undone.

Interconnected defects mark recent British school education.
The system overall is excessively reliant on public finance and
public provision. Since the Second World War, educational policy
has been driven by an administrative elite, of a fairly hetero-

geneous kind but united in its doctrinal commitment to public finance and public provision. Secondly, British education is highly centralized, at all levels from infant teaching to postgraduate university work. This is typical of public sector organizations whose personnel always have a strong interest in centralization. There is a tendency among senior personnel to pursue private goals to the exclusion or diminution of their official public functions. A public servant who is supposed to be facilitating teaching and learning, but who instead pursues income or power or to promote a more equal society, is effectively substituting his/her pleasure for duty. Political initiatives get frustrated in operation. The elaborate 'National Curriculum' ushered in by the 1988 Education Act is a case in point. Given the dismal cognitive standards in schools, this had been intended to improve things by means of simple English and Mathematics teaching. In the hands of the education elite, however, it became unsuccessful, the victim of a giant bureaucracy. The entire framework of intellectual life in the primary and secondary schools has to be centralized, planned with a kind of Soviet-style conceit. Centralization permits the intensification and protection of elite power. Central control facilitates the creation of barriers to entry in particular areas of production and thus maintains that power.

In education, central control is used to define what counts as a qualified teacher, what is to be regarded as acceptable teaching, and what constitutes adequate appraisal of the work done by pupils and students. These three – curriculum, pedagogy and appraisal – are the main constituents of educational transmission. Effectively, monopoly powers in education accrue to the group of bureaucrats, politicos and academics who control this transmission. Monopolistic powers arise from this method of finance and centralization.

It is not too much to call the present predicament a crisis, one especially telling index being the alienation and disillusionment of teachers, at primary, secondary and tertiary level. In secondary schools this has now been very effectively charted by the new NUT-Cambridge study of April 2004. Secondary teachers are faced with high workloads, inspections, large classes and new initiatives; the largest issue is the pandemic of badly behaved and hard to control children.[2] Such behaviour has many causes. But it is in part an outcome of a stern moral order having been replaced by a very relaxed one or nothing at all. It reflects failure of educationists to grasp crucial links between learning *morals* and learning *generally*.[3] There is little discourse or reflection on such crucial moral prerequisites for learning as diligence, perseverance, obedience and courage.

Elementary education was sucked into the orbit of the state in the late nineteenth century. It is not possible to come to know what an entire public really wants educationally. Even in the case of those who do not sullenly accept what they are given, real educational preferences are not readily discernible, since they lie submerged in a deep sea of the public sector. Once preferences are subsidized thus, it becomes impossible to know what people's educational preferences are. The nationalization of education – the mix of compulsory attendance and public funding and provision – caused a huge and until now permanent transfer of educational power from the demand side of production, to the suppliers, not the broad mass of teachers, but the educational bureaucracy. G. K. Chesterton pointed out 'Jones' had lost the right to a say in his children's education. A lot of people who should have noticed this disastrous transfer today have still not done so. Not knowing people's wants, nor caring about them, the educational establishment has for long tended to substitute its own preferences. The bigger the scale of educational enrolment and the more intellectually complex the various levels of the curriculum become, the more intractable becomes the problem of sorting out real educational priorities.

Problems have been heightened at tertiary level for twenty years now, by a deliberate policy of very rapid expansion of numbers, coupled with a much older policy, now stretching back forty years, of advised intention to reduce per capita costs in real terms. The weaker universities do not reach proper standards. Low intellectual standards in many of these tertiary institutions have a reinforcing impact on inadequate standards further down the hierarchy, the levels of achievement required to gain entry to such places being pitifully low.

The 1960s was the crucial decade. Before then, however unsatisfactory it may have been for the public to lose virtually all discretion over educational policy, the elite was well-meaning. The institutionalization of socialist ideologies has meant the education sector in this country now bears a strong, systemic resemblance to defunct Soviet-type economies of Communist times. Our education system today is a kind of writ-small socialism. The 1980s in no sense dented the power of the educational elite who emerged from them stronger than ever.

Until the late 1950s, the scale of education was rather modest. Few people went to university and even the numbers staying on past the official leaving age of fifteen years were comparatively small. The cult of equality was in its infancy, though the destruction of the grammar schools and the obligation for all children outside the private sector to go to comprehensive secondary schools was under way. In the late 1960s the drive towards comprehensive schools intensified. While we owe the survival of our 180 remaining grammar schools to the Thatcher Government, the process of 'comprehensivization' did not get reversed. The Conservatives did little to restrain the in-house ideologies of the educational elite. Not only were grammar schools and their facilitating instrument, the eleven-plus examination, largely abolished; simultaneously primary education abandoned streaming and whole-class teaching and adopted generally the child-centred approach to learning. Children must be regarded as 'equal' to each other, whatever their range of abilities, and children as a category must be considered of equal importance with the adult category. The notoriously bad behaviour of many young people in this country today reflects a deliberate erosion of adult authority, championed in the name of 'progress', as witnessed in the disastrous phrase *progressive education*. To compound the faults effected by the treating of very young people as if they were mature, those many brave and worthy teachers who have struggled to reimpose moral order in school have found themselves increasingly hampered in their attempts at disciplining unruly children. Naughty children are now as hard to get rid of as bad teachers.

We have said that lack of moral training and weak educational performance are linked issues. In fact, low intellectual standards and bad discipline are related to the progressive mind-set. If the trade-off is between children's being strongly disciplined and educationally accomplished on the one hand, and very relaxed and unconcerned over authority and educationally impoverished on the other, many progressives would plump for the latter combination. In fact we can observe similar preferences across the whole of social policy. The point is that we will not get far in the matter of standards if we do not grasp that for progressive education they do not count for much.

Thus, much of the debate about standards is in a crucial sense irrelevant. If more and more boys and girls are to stay in school rather than work, if more and more young people are to go to university, lower *average* standards must result. In the case of tertiary education, for forty years governments have maintained a deliberate policy of lowering unit costs for undergraduate education. If average ability has gone down and average funding too, what conclusion could possibly be drawn other than that standards are down and that the process was brought about by deliberate policy?

Let us even so dwell a while on the sort of argument employed in defence of the case that general educational standards are not lower than before. The proven illiteracy and innumeracy we now have are manifest evidence of a vast economic inefficiency, since it is incontestable that spending on education has increased more or less continuously in real terms for decades. In other words, even if standards are stationary, *educational productivity* has slumped catastrophically.

Far from being reversed in the Thatcher years, this whole socialist apparatus underwent a further marked hypertrophy. With the introduction in 1988 of the National Curriculum, the closest approximation to a Leninist political apparatus in the whole of British history, we were given an extraordinary demonstration of the economic ignorance of the educational elite. Our national educational faults work in combination to give British education in its various national contexts – England and Wales, Scotland, and Northern Ireland – its special character. Education is supply-driven. An elite group of the suppliers have captured the curriculum, pedagogy and examinations. Education has become a kind of socialist, intellectual fifth column, reinforced at tertiary level by a large enrolment in soft social science and ideologically corrupted arts, whose influence radiates down the system.

The central economic problem of British education is that we do not know what the population's educational preferences are, since they have been trodden down roughshod, or obscured by government. Once intellectual transmission is publicly financed it becomes impossible to tell who wants what, and in what amounts and to what level. Because parents do not pay directly but only via taxation for education, they tend to see it as costless. A kind of frivolity obtains when people are spending the money of others, or constrained by others who are doing so. It is also often difficult in the context of publicly financed intellectual production even to distinguish demand for subject matter from the supply of it, so opaque does the economic milieu become. Often those who teach and sometimes those who learn, race relations, 'gender' studies, greenery, soft sociology of various kinds, etc. are engaged in a kind of collective consumerism. The presence of others, non-consumers, is largely coerced, and often ineffectually so there is a vast truancy in secondary schools in particular, most of it curricular or pedagogic in nature. It is worth dwelling a little more on the kind of curricular calculus which obtains when people's educational arrangements are publicly financed and provided.

One way of treating expenditure is through the three categories 'consumption, investment and waste'. The balance between these three is distorted when flows of private spending are displaced.

A purchase is consumption when it is intended to satisfy present wants. It is investment when it is aimed at increasing future abilities to consume. It is waste when it satisfies neither of these purposes. The hypothetical question concerns 'raw' preferences. In educational matters the question is actually *counterfactual*, certainly in the British instance, since preferences are far from raw, having been processed by the intervention of politicians and bureaucrats. This being so, it may be asserted that for many pupils the curriculum encourages additional *consumption*. Many prefer the undemanding calls of soft social science to the harsh imperatives of mathematics or physics. It is hard not to see the rise of the soft social sciences, and the enormous enrolment in sociology at the tertiary level, as a giant curricular consumption spree, whereby, in the last few decades, millions of students and many thousands of teachers have been playing fast and loose with the taxpayer's money. The softening of discipline and the advised lowering of standards have worked in the same direction. A system tending to low-level curricular consumerism and extensive waste tends to dispense low moral and intellectual standards.

Much of the failure of our educational arrangements is also facilitated on the supply side by the introduction of wrong systems of teaching of reading and mathematics. Many children are unable to cope with either consumption or investment. In other words, a shocking element of waste is built into the system itself. Political leaders do not seem to understand the dire effects of public finance and public provision. This is not because it is beyond them. Rather it might be represented as 'beneath' them. They have simply never thought about it. Today, however, education is the most important item of national discussion. Intellectual corruption may be the worst form of all corruption.[4]

Even conservative observers have taken the view that once you nationalize education you effectively have the same curriculum and same pedagogy but everything merely gets done worse, everything malfunctions; education does the right things, but it does them badly. The reality is otherwise. Things are not just done worse, they are also done differently. Public finance and provision give you a different curriculum, different teaching and different examinations from what private finance would generate. It can be pathological in content and emphasis; even dysfunctional in having preoccupations which would not meet sober public approval. How many primary schoolchildren have now been taught that resources are running out, and so on? Such claims are dubious where they are not false. How many undergraduates have been confidently assured that there are no differences between the sexes other than those attributable to social construction?

Paradoxically, if you scraped off the patina of Marxism from the curriculum in say Poland or Hungary under Communism, underneath was an old fashioned European curriculum. And it was imposed without let or hindrance, by an elite which *endorsed* the political order. In the free societies educational arrangements are largely controlled by an elite which *opposes* the general political order, but which also mimics in some degree the genuine freedoms which Western society permits.

There are two principal modes of educational regulation with regard to the publicly financed education of the free societies. One is a pale copy of Communist management. Stanislaw Andreski dubbed it bureaucratic centralism. Its best example is the British National Curriculum; it has been a failure and it may be a good thing it has been largely unravelled and looks set for definitive remaindering. The other is less well known and probably has a great future, since it imitates the freedoms of modernity. We may call it 'subsidized innovation' – the controlling elite improvises on the basis of money raised from taxation. These improvisations have effects on curriculum, pedagogy and evaluation at all levels. Characteristic of such improvisations is that the public are not consulted. Take the abandonment of streaming in primary schools. This was a pure function of elite preference. It would have been unthinkable had the public been consulted and doubly so if they had had to pay directly for it. Take the dropping of whole-class teaching, and rote learning of spelling and tables: again, nothing but elite preference. So too was the removal of the vital exercise of précis from the secondary school curriculum. At the same time, there has been institutionalized resistance in schools and in teacher education alike, to the best methods, for example of teaching reading and maths, despite a rhetoric of 'best practice'. There has also been persecution of non-conformists.

It needs to be said again that low intellectual and moral standards are not accidental features of our education. Doubtless many teachers acted in good faith when they effectively tore up the traditional moral rule book. Perhaps they thought liberation would flow from these changes. It is hard not to see them as deliberately conceived in some quarters as ways of increasing antagonism to the existing moral order. Nor is it accidental that the context of all this is public finance and public provision. There is a very strong case for the view that had these innovations required private expenditures they would not have happened. Part of our tragic impasse at present is that though there is a widespread dissatisfaction with our educational arrangements the public is habituated to public finance and public provision. One day the link between the two will presumably be understood.

Another example of wayward innovation was the destruction of the excellent General Certificate of Education, first at the Ordinary Level and latterly at the Advanced Level. The destruction of the GCE ranks with the destruction of the grammar schools as an act of intellectual barbarism. Arrangements which were excellent were abandoned because too many children could not cope with them. Why not keep them and devise less demanding ones for less able children, rather than levelling the whole structure downwards? These changes have today dropped our children and teachers into a wilderness of low standards, blatant grade manipulation and widespread cheating. One result of this has been that our examination grades have lost much of their quasi-pricing function, their value as hiring information for employers.

Think too of the tendentious language of educational theorizing. We were told from the 1960s that there was nothing wrong with the culture of the masses of children and that it was 'elitist' to try to rectify it. It was repeated loudly that there is no such thing as 'cultural deprivation', when in reality the phrase fairly describes half or more of our entire population. These manoeuvres of language have been employed as yet another weapon in the war against education. It was in the 1980s that the phrase about children needing to 'own the curriculum' became common currency. In fact the only way to give parents and other 'consumers' of education effective rights over the curriculum is to allow their demands to be the crucial element in deciding what happens in schools and colleges.

In reality, for the most part nobody owns the curriculum nor the pedagogy. The educational elite control them, just as they also control the examination system. They do not own them or want to. They could be owned only if there were property rights which rewarded the educational successes of the owners of educational institutions and penalized their failures. The rent-seeking elite do not want the responsibility and restriction which would attend such opportunity. They want control without responsibility. They want to privatize decision-making only, in favour of their own decisions; the costs they want socialized. This posture explains why study methods are taught in the lesser universities. It is because they were not taught, as they should be, in schools, further down the system. It explains why the army of 'Special Needs' is so vast in primary and secondary education. It is because the initial curriculum and pedagogy are so poorly conceived and so poorly delivered and the examinations which should steer and correct them are so feeble. All this amounts to taxpayers picking up the social costs of the systemic failure which is bound to happen when wrong ideologies of education, wrong technical methods and wrong attitudes to private enterprise are institutionalized in schools.

The elite have children of their own. They have also recruited to their ideology a sizeable element of the middle classes. By now there are whole generations actually raised in the soft sociology culture, people whose mind-set is in the grip of what, without disapproval, the late Basil Bernstein called 'a closed and explicit ideology'.[5] This causes a huge distortion in educational decision-making. Because the parents, teachers and older students and educational administrators involved are using the resources of the taxpayer, rather than their own, the balance between curricular investment and consumption is drastically tipped towards the latter. People study soft subjects for the buzz, rather than under-taking the hard grind of mathematics. Some get to university to read degrees in English, where instead of Shakespeare and Milton they spend their days reading French nihilism. On top of this expensive dysfunctional fare, there is also waste on a truly colossal scale: millions of citizens ending up illiterate or innumerate after eleven years of compulsory school. This is the evidence of educational malfunction.

Even the educational elite know things are in chaos. This is indexed by the endless progression of ineffectual or counter-productive reforms and spurious initiatives, often decked out in pompous changes of language, to which our schools and colleges have been subject. The Education Ministry itself has been subjected to pointless and misconceived changes of name. The 'Department of Education and Science' was a reasonable title. 'Department of Education and Employment' was an ignorant and philistine one, wrongly implying that employment is an *aim* of education, when in fact employment is only an important functional by-product of education. Similarly, 'Department for Education and Skills' ministers to the skills lobby, a pressure group which has done much to disorientate our educational purposes. Philosophically, education is about the pursuit of knowledge and virtue, and 'skills' are subsumed at an elementary level in the search for education, not separate from it.

Just as during the death of Communism, those asked to reform it were the ones who had most to lose, so reform of our education has always been entrusted to the very people who would lose by it, since they gain from present imperfections and faults. The result is that education and the commercial economy have been left radically out of kilter. It is surely preposterous that in one of the richest countries in the world there is only one private university and that less than 10 per cent of our boys and girls are privately educated. Marxist sociology of education took the education system as a bourgeois control apparatus. This carries the implication that the actions of teachers and the curriculum and examinations to which children are subjected, function to reproduce the capitalist class structure. The children are differentially socialized for different roles in an oppressive, alienating division of labour. It is actually as Basil Bernstein himself partly divined, an interrupter apparatus, which by changing the curriculum and pedagogy of schools according to its own 'progressive' dynamic, alters the beliefs and composition of the social hierarchy. 'A closed and specific ideology' had been institutionalized. This closure was imposed on a helpless populace, not by popular demand but entirely by supply-side fiat. Again, let us repeat that it seems inconceivable such obscurantism would have been favoured by a consulted and paying public. Today we must go far beyond Bernstein, who expressed no hostility to the phenomenon he had noticed. Conservatives and libertarians, by contrast, though they will tolerate the existence of socialist ideology, will not view with favour a mode of finance which encourages and fortifies these disastrous outlooks.

Notes

1   The difference between public finance and public provision is defined by vouchers in education. Vouchers would provide public finance but private provision of education. The locus classicus is Milton Friedman. See www.friedmanfoundation.org/.

   The voucher case has never got very far in Britain. It is still a form of public finance and it was always likely that the state would intrude sooner or later if it was putting up the funds. Vouchers would facilitate exit, and thus diminish producer-capture somewhat. They do not do anything about the worst feature of state education, that it is compulsory. Maybe the externalities involved make this necessary but I am still sceptical. Millions of children leave primary school and secondary school illiterate and innumerate both in America and the United Kingdom. The best-known book is Arthur

Seldon's *The Riddle of the Voucher: An Inquiry into the Obstacles to Introducing Choice and Competition in State Schools* (London: Institute of Economic Affairs, 1986). Seldon tersely recounted the failure of the voucher movement in this country. According to Seldon, 'Experiments in the voucher system were suppressed in 1983 largely because it was opposed by vested interests, mainly in the teacher trade unions.' Arthur Seldon, 'The Verdict of History' in Arthur Seldon (ed.) *Reprivatising Welfare after the Lost Century* (IEA, 1996, pp. 109–10).

2   John MacBeath and Maurice Galton with Susan Steward, Charlotte Page and Janet Edwards, *A Life in Secondary Teaching: Finding Time for Learning*, Report Commissioned by the National Union of Teachers, concerning workloads in Secondary Schools, 2004.

3   Dennis O'Keeffe, 'Diligence Abandoned: the Dismissal of Traditional Virtues in the School', in Digby Anderson (ed.) *The Loss of Virtue: Moral Confusion and Social Disorder in Britain and America* (The Social Affairs Unit/A National Review Book, 1992).

4   David Marsland, *Seeds of Bankruptcy: Sociological Bias against Business and Freedom* (Claridge, 1988); Dennis O'Keeffe, *Political Correctness and Public Finance* (IEA, 1999).

5   Basil Bernstein, *Class, Codes and Control* (Routledge and Kegan Paul, 1977, vol. 3).

8 Market solutions for school education

James Tooley and James Stanfield

All over the world, governments are seeing the private sector as a driver of modernization and progress in education. This is so for four main reasons. First, across the world, there have been doubts about the effectiveness and efficiency of public education. Secondly, there are doubts about the equity, or fairness, of public education, and its accountability, especially to the disadvantaged and poor. Thirdly, there is an increasing awareness of initiatives by educational entrepreneurs, and evidence to suggest that competitive pressures can lead to significant educational improvements. Fourthly, a practical consideration is the need to restrain public expenditure, in order to reduce budget deficits and external debts, and the consequent need to find alternative sources of educational funding.

If we want to create a world-class system, then it is to the world that we should turn for possible solutions. There are market solutions found throughout the world and these can be usefully classified into three normative types: *alternative funding* (universal and targeted vouchers, tax credits), *alternative schools* (publicly funded private/independent schools); and *alternative providers* (contracting out state school management to the private sector).

Alternative funding

An education voucher (originally championed by Milton Friedman in 1962 and rejected by the late Sir Keith Joseph in 1984) is a coupon provided by government for parents to spend with an

135

education provider of their choice, within limits set by government. These can be universal or targeted for particular groups. The only two countries with universal vouchers are Sweden and Chile, while there are several targeted schemes in countries as diverse as the USA, Bangladesh and Colombia. Since 1992, municipalities in Sweden have been obliged to give 85 per cent of the average cost per pupil to any school of parental choice – for all pupils. The figure of 85 per cent was calculated so as to give *equal* funding to the independent schools, with the other 15 per cent accounting for the overheads and administration of the municipalities. The figure was reduced to 75 per cent in 1995. A rapid growth of private schools has been experienced since these reforms were introduced. Enrolment in independent schools ranges from 0 per cent to nearly 20 per cent in municipalities, with about 10 per cent in Stockholm. Municipality views on the appropriateness of new independent schools are taken into account by the National Agency for Education (NAE), but they must, by law, finance any private school that has been approved by the NAE. As long as schools fulfil certain basic requirements, *any* kind of school is eligible, from religious schools to those run by for-profit corporations. This has led to the growth of three chains of for-profit private schools. One of these is Kunskapsskolan ('The Knowledge School'), which currently operates twelve schools, with 2,800 pupils. Within the next five years, Kunskapsskolan is expected to operate 50 schools with 20,000 pupils all over Sweden.

In America the most famous targeted voucher schemes are in Milwaukee and Cleveland. The Milwaukee Parent Choice Program (MPCP) was introduced in 1990, specifically targeting low-income families. The voucher's value is set at the per-pupil rate at government schools. Parents qualify for a voucher only if their family income is no more than 1.75 times the official poverty level. In 1998 the growth of the programme burgeoned, when the Wisconsin Supreme Court ruled that religious schools could participate in the programme, a decision endorsed by the US Supreme Court in 2002. The Cleveland voucher programme is similar, enacted in 1995 with legislation modelled on the Milwaukee system. Religious schools can participate in the programme, and children who were currently attending private schools could apply. Families with incomes below the poverty line received 90 per cent of tuition fees and those above the cut-off point 75 per cent of the tuition fees. In its first year, the programme was limited to 2,000 pupils. By the end of 1996 this target had been met – with 55 private schools operating the voucher scheme.

An alternative approach, the *Florida A+ Plan for Education*, targets *failure* of state schools, rather than poverty. The programme provides vouchers to children in a government school that is graded F twice in a period of four years. The programme was introduced in June 1999 and became the first State-wide voucher programme to be implemented in the USA. The idea is that schools will improve their performance owing to the fear of being shamed into closing or losing pupils and revenue. The value of the voucher is a maximum of $4,000, to be spent in any private or government school.

Educational tax credits can take three main forms: non-refundable (where a family has cost of education subtracted from its tax payment), refundable (where a sum more than one's tax burden can be claimed) and finally where businesses or philanthropically minded individuals can also fund a disadvantaged child's private education, and count this contribution against their tax liability. The first US States to introduce tax credits were Minnesota and Arizona in 1997, followed by Iowa in 1998, Illinois in 1999 and Pennsylvania in 2001. In Illinois and Iowa the State matches 25 per cent of the parental contribution in tax credit, but only up to a maximum of $500 in Illinois and $250 in Iowa. In Pennsylvania corporations can receive tax credits to the amount of 75 per cent of their contributions. In Minnesota, the scheme allows a $1,000 tax credit per pupil for families with incomes up to $37,500. Tax credits can be used for private tutoring, textbooks, school transport, computers and instructional materials, but not for school fees. Families with incomes above this level receive a tax *deduction* of up to $2,500 for private school fees, as well as the other expenses that are covered under the tax credit.

In all of the States apart from Minnesota and Arizona, tax credits can be set against tuition costs. All States allow the claim to be made against materials and other forms of schooling, apart from Arizona. The majority of the tax credit schemes are not means tested, although the maximum value of the tax credit is stated in each State. In Arizona taxpayers receive a dollar-for-dollar tax credit when they donate to scholarship organizations providing support for students who attend or wish to attend private school. Taxpayers can make individual donation of up to $500 per year, and a married couple $625 per year. This has led, between 1998–2000, to donations of approximately $32 million generated by these educational tax credits, funding 19,000 scholarships.

The Canadian Province of Ontario is also introducing a tax credit scheme. The scheme will allow a qualifying taxpayer to claim a tax credit of a certain percentage of eligible tuition fees paid to an eligible independent school. Starting in 2002 taxpayers can claim 10 per cent of fees, rising 10 per cent each year until 50 per cent can be claimed in 2006. Finally, several European countries also have tax deductions for private education. In Germany, for instance, parents who send their children to (subsidized) private schools are eligible for certain allowances against tax including: an amount for a child at boarding school; 30 per cent of the cost of all school fees; and transport costs.

Alternative schools

A common approach, particularly in the European Union, is for the encouragement of choice and diversity in education through the state subsidy of private schools. Such an approach is also found in the charter schools in America and in Hong Kong. A scheme ensuring freedom of parental choice in education in the Netherlands has been in operation for almost 100 years, enshrined in the constitution of 1917. Altogether about 70 per cent of children attend private schools – of which the majority are church schools, with a total of 7 per cent at non-religious private schools. Schools include Montessori and Steiner, together with Jewish, Islamic, Hindu and humanist schools.

There is ease of entry for new suppliers. Any group of parents or other interested parties can make application to the Ministry of Education, Culture and Science to establish a new school. The number of parents required to open a school varies with the size of the municipality, from 50 parents in small municipalities (fewer than 25,000 people) to 125 in municipalities with more than 100,000 people. If successful in their application, these groups are *guaranteed* to receive state funding to set up and maintain their private school. Capital and recurrent costs for the school, including the buildings, are supplied by the state. All government and private grant-aided schools are guaranteed the same financial support. Interestingly, although private schools are not allowed to charge top-up fees, they are allowed to receive contributions from parents to fund the purchase of teaching materials, fund extracurricular activities, employ additional staff or pay teachers a supplement to their regular salaries. These 'fees' range from $100 to $200 per year at most primary schools, higher at secondary schools.

Denmark shares with the Netherlands the key feature that there is a constitutional right for parents to set up their own schools and receive state funding. Currently, about 12 per cent of primary and lower-secondary pupils are in the private sector, and 5 per cent of upper-secondary pupils. Twenty-one per cent of schools at the primary and lower-secondary level are in the private sector. Since the Free School Act of 1855, parents and organizations have been able to set up their own schools. Any private organization or group of adults or parents can set up a private school for children between six and eighteen years of age. To receive government funding, the minimum size of primary or lower-secondary private schools is only 28 pupils after three years: with at least 12 pupils enrolled in the first year, 20 in the second year and from then on, 28 pupils. All approved private schools are entitled to receive state subsidies covering approximately 80 per cent of their operational expenditure on the basis of the number of pupils enrolled at the individual school in a given year, plus a capital allowance, and other special grants. On top of these grants, parents pay a moderate fee. At primary and lower-secondary level, parents pay DKK 8,100 a year per pupil on average, or about 19 per cent of the total expenditure. At upper-secondary level, parents pay on average DKK 10,400 a year per pupil.

In Germany private education is growing at a remarkable rate. This is fastest in the east German *Länder*, where private schools, first allowed only in 1990, had grown to some 154 by 1998. In the west German *Länder*, growth of around 14 per cent has been experienced between 1992 and 1998. At the *Gymnasium* (lower- and upper-secondary school), 10.3 per cent of pupils are in the private sector, and there are 11.3 per cent of schools in the private sector at this level. For *Realschule*, the level is 7.1 per cent of pupils (7.7 per cent of schools); special schools are 16.4 per cent in the private sector. So at certain levels of schooling, private education even in Germany is significantly higher than in the UK. In terms of financing, the *Land* governments 'are required to ensure private schools' existence' under constitutional entitlements. In practice, all of the *Länder* provide subsidies to private schools, provided that they are non-profit bodies. Such financial support includes subsidies for staffing costs, and is usually a lump sum comparable to that in the state schools. In addition, there are subsidies to cover construction costs, textbooks and teachers' pension funds. Importantly, private schools are allowed to charge fees, to cover their extra costs. They are also not required to follow the same timetables or curricula as public sector schools, and are also free to choose their textbooks. They are free to promote religious or philosophical views, and use teaching methods of their own choice. Moreover, private schools have complete freedom to hire and fire teaching staff, and inspection is fairly minimal.

In Hong Kong an interesting form of state subsidy has emerged, reinforced and extended since the colony reverted to China. Here, fee paying school places are provided for about 85 per cent of the

15-year-old cohort. Importantly, publicly funded private schools are permitted to charge fees. And to counteract the argument that the introduction of school fees will exclude children from low-income families, the Hong Kong government introduced a Fee Remission Policy. This is designed to channel a percentage of funds collected from fees into the subsidized places for the poor. While for-profit companies are allowed to operate schools, the majority of publicly funded schools in Hong Kong are owned and managed by churches, trusts and private organizations. Private schools that receive public funds are defined as Aided Schools and receive specific grants from the Department of Education for staff costs and all operating expenses. Grants that cover operating costs are calculated depending on the number of classes, students and subjects taught.

Perhaps the kind of public subsidy of private schools best-known (in Britain) are the Charter schools in the USA. Charter schools are free from direct administrative government control and are under fewer regulatory constraints than state schools. They must, however, meet the performance standards set by their charter. This freedom allows Charter schools to have more control over their curriculum, hours of operation, the staff they employ, budget and internal organization, schedule. The funding they receive is based upon the number of pupils in attendance – so fewer pupils means less funding. The concept was first introduced in 1991, in Minnesota, and by January 2000, there was charter legislation in 36 states, plus Washington DC, with over 500,000 pupils enrolled in Charter schools. During the 2000–01 school year there were 2069 Charter schools operating in America. Charter schools can be converted state schools, converted private schools, or new schools. In fact, about 70 per cent of Charter schools are brand-new schools. Charter schools are not allowed to charge tuition fees in any State, although it is possible to invite voluntary contributions from parents for building projects. In general, too, Charter schools can – and do – go bankrupt: they are not protected by the State from this happening, and will do so if they have not been able to attract sufficient pupils, or have poorly managed their budgets. In all States too, if there is excess demand for places – as there is in some 70 per cent of Charter schools – places are allocated by 'equitable means' such as a lottery. Three types of body have been attracted to the Charter school market:

- Charities seeking to promote a particular way of life, such as Heritage Academies promoting 'American values and civic pride'.
- Charities promoting improved education for disadvantaged or ignored groups.
- In 21 of the 36 states – including Arizona, Massachusetts and Michigan – for-profit companies which are allowed to manage Charter schools.

Alternative providers

The final type of market solution is to contract out education management to 'Alternative Providers', in particular, for-profit companies. Here we take the largest American operator as an exemplar of this trend, Edison Schools, which is significant in the British context: its interest in the UK market led to Surrey County Council's decision to contract out King's Manor School, the first school 'privatization' here. Edison is exploring the possibilities of entering the British market – although its recent sharp fall in share price may curtail this process again.

After spending three years of R&D, drawing on best practice and ideas from around the world on curriculum, technology and school organization, Edison created its educational model which was brought into its first four schools in 1995. It is now the USA's leading private manager of State schools – and the sixtieth largest 'school district', albeit the only national one. In the 2000–01 school year, Edison operated 108 schools in 21 States, with about 58,000 pupils. About one-third of Edison's schools are Charter schools, while the other two-thirds are under contract with the school districts. All Edison schools are schools of choice – that is, no parents are forced to send their children to them, and all parents can opt out of a school that becomes an Edison school.

In its contract schools, Edison negotiates with school districts to take over the management of (usually) its failing schools. It takes only the funding that would otherwise be available for these schools, on a per capita basis, and commits itself to implementing in full its comprehensive school design. This includes, amongst other elements:

- Schools have a longer day and year, adding the equivalent of more than six years of curriculum time for the typical American student.
- Teachers receive four weeks of training, and there is ongoing professional development.
- Assessment and monitoring of students is a priority, to ensure clear accountability to families and to the public, using state and district tests, benchmark assessments, structured portfolios, and quarterly learning contracts with parents.

A voucher proposal for England and Wales
Given the evidence from around the world a clear proposal emerges for England and Wales.[1] We propose a Swedish-style universal voucher plan for England and Wales, judiciously combining elements within it of the Danish, Dutch, German and Hong Kong private school subsidy systems. The voucher system has the following seven elements:

1. The basic model is that of Sweden. That is, the voucher can be used at any public or private school of the family's choice. As in Sweden, it is a universal voucher, for all children, including those who currently attend private school.
2. As in Sweden, local authorities (or any other authority) cannot object to any school receiving the parent voucher, providing that it has satisfied certain minimum standards.

3. As in the Netherlands and Denmark, schools can admit pupils according to any criteria they wish, including religious ones.

4. As in Sweden, any school provider will be allowed to participate in the voucher scheme, including charities, trusts, and for-profit providers.

5. As in Sweden and Denmark, the state subsidy need not be 100 per cent of the current state expenditure on schooling, but can be set *if necessary* at a slightly lower rate. The exact level of the subsidy would be determined when the level of surplus funding from DfES, QCA, Ofsted, etc., has been determined.

6. As in Germany and Hong Kong, top-up fees will be allowed to be charged by those schools in receipt of the state voucher.

7. As in Hong Kong, a special scholarship system will be constructed to allow the poorest to attend the private school of their choice.

As the global development of market solutions in education will now become the key driving force for future reforms in the UK, we may no longer have to depend upon UK politicians to think the unthinkable and blaze new trails. That said, there will still be the need to prepare for future change by continuing to highlight the absurdities inherent within the existing education system. Nowhere have such absurdities been better portrayed than in the TV comedy series *Yes Minister* and *Yes Prime Minister*, which were based upon the perception that there was a wide gap between the rhetoric of government and the realities of running a country, and that the gap was rich in comic potential. According to one of the scriptwriters, Sir Antony Jay: 'One of the most hilarious absurdities was education. The system rested on the denial of choice to all parents except the wealthy. Those who deplored this inequality sought to remove it not by expanding choice to the less well off but by denying it to the better off as well. The defence of the system rested on the absurd argument that politicians, educationists and officials know better than parents what education our children need unless they are in the top income bracket. The argument absolutely demanded a place in our comedy series.' Part of the script of that particular episode appears in the Appendix to this chapter, with Jim Hacker as Prime Minister, Sir Humphrey Appleby as Cabinet Secretary, and Dorothy Wainwright as the PM's Political Adviser.

For Sir Antony Jay the key lesson to be learnt from this episode is that if the state does intend to assist in the financing of education then the fatal error is to subsidize the producer and not the consumer: 'Giving money to schools not only takes all effective choice away from citizens, it also creates a massive bureaucratic superstructure of inspectors, auditors, committee advisers and administrators, with an accompanying blizzard of regulations, guidelines, consultative documents, reports and instructions which practically bring the cost of educating a child up to the levels of good private schools, which manage without these bureaucratic luxuries. By contrast, giving the money to parents restores their choice and creates competition between schools – competition that is far more effective in raising standards than bureaucratic control and regulatory frameworks'.[2] The above reference to the critical role of competition in education would have found particular favour with an ardent fan of *Yes Prime Minister*, the late F. A. Hayek, who defined competition as a process in which people acquire and communicate knowledge. Education without competition would therefore appear to be a contradiction in terms.

Appendix: *Yes Prime Minister* – 'The National Education Service'

Antony Jay and Jonathan Lynn[3]

I called Humphrey in first thing this morning. Dorothy was with me. I tried to disguise my excitement as I casually told him that I wanted to bounce a new idea off him.

The word 'new' usually alerts Humphrey that trouble's in store, but this time he seemed perfectly relaxed and actually chuckled when I told him that I've realized how to reform our education system.

So I let him have it. 'Humphrey, I'm going to let parents take their children away from schools. They will be able to move them to any school they want.'

He was unconcerned. 'You mean, after application, scrutiny, tribunal hearing and appeal procedures?'

It was my turn to chuckle. 'No, Humphrey. They could just move them. Whenever they want.'

'I'm sorry, Prime Minister, I don't follow you.' I could see that he genuinely didn't understand.

Dorothy spelled it out, abrasively. 'The government, Sir Humphrey, is going to let parents decide which school to send their children to.'

Suddenly he understood that we actually meant what we were saying. He exploded into protest. 'Prime Minister, you're not serious?'

I nodded benevolently. 'Yes I am.'

'But that's preposterous!'

'Why?' asked Dorothy.

He ignored her completely. 'You can't let parents make these choices. How on earth would parents know which schools are best?'

Coolly I appraised him. 'What school did you go to, Humphrey?'

'Winchester.'

'Was it good?' I asked politely.

'Excellent, of course.'

'Who chose it?'

'My parents, naturally.' I smiled at him. 'Prime Minister, that's quite different. My parents were discerning people. You can't expect *ordinary* people to know where to send their children.'

Dorothy was manifestly shocked at Humphrey's snobbery and elitism. 'Why on earth not?'

He shrugged. The answer was obvious to him. 'How could they tell?'

Dorothy, a mother herself, found the question only too easy to answer. 'They could tell if their kids could read and write and do sums. They could tell if the neighbours were happy with the school. They could tell if the exam results aren't good.'

Again he studiously ignored her. 'Examination Prime Minister.'

Dorothy stood up, moved around the Cabinet table and sat down very close to me so that Humphrey could no longer avoid meeting her eyes. 'That is true, Humphrey – and those parents who don't want an academic education for their kids could choose progressive schools.'

I could see that, as far as Humphrey was concerned, Dorothy and I were talking ancient Chinese. He simply didn't understand us. Again he tried to explain his position, and he was becoming quite emotional. 'Parents are not qualified to make these choices. Teachers are the professionals. In fact, parents are the worst people to bring up children, they have no qualifications for it. We don't allow untrained teachers to teach. The same would apply to parents in an ideal world.'

I realized with stunning clarity, and for the very first time, how far Humphrey's dream of an ideal world differed from mine. 'You mean,' I asked slowly and quietly, 'parents should be stopped from having kids until they've been trained?'

He sighed impatiently. Apparently I'd missed the point. – 'No, no. Having kids isn't the problem. They've all been trained to *have* kids, sex education classes have been standard for years now.'

'I see,' I said, and turned to Dorothy, who was wide-eyed in patent disbelief at our most senior Civil Servant and advocate of the Orwellian corporate state. 'Perhaps,' I suggested, 'we can improve on the sex education classes? Before people have children we could give them exams. Written and practical. Or both, perhaps? Then we could issue breeding licences.'

Humphrey wasn't a bit amused. He ticked me off. 'There's no need to be facetious, Prime Minister. I'm being serious. It's *looking after* children that parents are not qualified for. That's why they have no idea how to choose schools for them. It couldn't work.'

Humphrey was now in full flow, passionate, emotional, scathing, committed like I have never seen. '. . . Prime Minister, we're discussing education. And with respect Prime Minister, I think you should know that the Department of Education and Science will react with some caution to this rather novel proposal.'

This was the language of war! Humphrey had all guns blazing. I've never heard such abusive language from him.

I stayed calm. 'So you think they'll block it?'

'I mean', he said, tight-lipped and angry, 'that they will give it the most serious and urgent consideration, but will insist on a thorough and rigorous examination of all the proposals, allied to a detailed feasibility study and budget analysis before producing a consultative document for consideration by all interested bodies and seeking comments and recommendations to be incorporated in a brief for a series of working parties who will produce individual studies that will form the background for a more wide-ranging document considering whether or not the proposal should be taken forward to the next stage.'

He meant they'd block it! But it will be no problem. No problem at all. Because, as I told him, I have a solution to that. 'So I'll abolish the Department of Education and Science!' I mentioned casually.

He thought he'd misheard. 'I'm sorry?'

'We'll abolish it,' I repeated obligingly.

'Abolish it?' He couldn't grasp the meaning of the words.

'Why not?' Dorothy wanted to see if there were any reason.

'Why not?' he said, his voice rising to the pitch of a Basil Fawlty at the end of his tether. 'Abolish Education and Science? It would be the end of civilization as we know it.'

I shook my head at him. He was quite hysterical. 'No, we'd only be abolishing the Department. Education and science will flourish.'

'Without a government department?' He was staring at us in horror, as though we were certifiably insane. 'Impossible!'

Dorothy seemed almost sorry for him. She tried to explain. 'Humphrey, government departments are tombstones. The Department of Industry marks the grave of industry. The Department of Employment marks the grave of employment. The Department of the Environment marks the grave of the environment. And the Department of Education marks where the corpse of British education is buried.'

He was staring the Goths and the Vandals in the face. He had no reply. So I asked him why we need the Department of Education and Science. What does it do? What's its role?

He tried to calm down and explain. 'I . . . I hardly know where to begin,' he began. 'It lays down guidelines, it centralizes and channels money to the Local Education Authorities and the University Grants Committee. It sets standards.'

I asked him a string of questions. 'Does it lay down the curriculum?'

'No, but . . .'

'Does it select and change Head Teachers?'

'No, but . . .'

'Does it maintain school buildings?'

'No, but . . .'

'Does it set and mark exams?'

'No, but . . .'

'Does it select the children?'

'No, but . . .'

'Then how', I wanted to know, 'does the Secretary of State affect how *my* child does at *her* school?'

To Humphrey the answer was obvious. 'He supplies sixty per cent of the cash!'

So that's it. We were right. Dorothy pursued the cross-examination. 'Why can't the cash go straight from the Treasury to the schools? And straight to the University Grants Committee? Do we really need 2,000 civil servants simply to funnel money from A to B?'

Almost in despair, he shook his head and cried: 'The Department of Education and Science also creates a legislative framework for education.'

What did he mean? There's hardly any legislation at all. What there is, the Department of the Environment could do – Environment deals with other local government matters.

Humphrey was fighting a desperate rearguard action. 'Prime Minister, you *can't* be serious. Who would assess forward planning and staffing variations, variations in pupil population, the density of schooling required in urban and rural areas . . . Who would make sure everything *ran properly*?'

'It doesn't run properly now,' I pointed out. 'Let's see if we can do better without the bureaucracy.'

'But who would plan for the future?'

I laughed. But I didn't just laugh, I laughed uproariously. Laughter overwhelmed me, for the first time since I'd been Prime Minister. Tears were rolling down my cheeks. 'Do you mean?' I finally gasped, breathless, weeping with laughter, 'that education in Britain today is what the Department of Education *planned*?'

'Yes, of course,' said Humphrey, and then went immediately and without hesitation straight into reverse. 'No, certainly not.'

Dorothy was getting bored with the meeting. She stood up. 'Two thousand five hundred private schools seem to solve these planning problems every day,' she commented curtly. 'They just respond to changing circumstances, supply and demand. Easy.'

I wanted to give Humphrey one last chance. 'Is there anything else the Department of Education and Science does?'

His eyes whizzed back and forth, as he thought furiously. 'Um . . . er. . . um.'

I stood up too. 'Fine,' I said. 'That's it. We don't need it, do we? Quod erat demonstrandum.'

Notes

1   See James Tooley, Pauline Dixon, James Stanfield (2003) *Delivering Better Education: Market Solutions for Educational Improvement* (London: Adam Smith Institute).

2   Antony Jay in James Tooley and James Stanfield (eds) *Government Failure: E. G. West on Education* (London: Institute of Economic Affairs, 2003).

3   Originally appeared as *Yes Prime Minister*, 'The National Education Service', series 2, no. 7, 1988, reprinted by kind permission of Antony Jay and Jonathan Lynn.

9 Private funding of science and higher education

Terence Kealey

Margaret Thatcher may have been Britain's only Prime Minister with a science degree herself. Her enthusiasm for British scientific creativity may have been unmatched, going hand in hand with her beliefs in free markets and risk-taking entrepreneurship. She distinctly promoted the Silicon Chip and spoke of the impending information technology revolution well before any other politician, for example in 1979 at the Cambridge Science Park.[1] In 1998 (well after retirement) she kept up the same: 'It's going to be more and more difficult to keep the truth out because of the Internet', she told the World Congress on Information Technology. She seemed to favour being seen at the cutting edge of science/technology – as if these went together with her other values.

Yet there were unresolved paradoxes and contradictions in her attitude towards science, free markets and the nature of research and higher education. 'Britain needs more Nobel prizes,' Mrs Thatcher said at a reception in London in the late 1980s. 'As many as Russia?' she was asked. She threw her interlocutor a cool look.

As Prime Minister she acquired a reputation as a cutter of British science budgets. But in fact British government support for academic science rose in real terms by about 30 per cent over her tenure as Prime Minister, with much of the increase taking place in the second part of her Premiership. The rate of increase was lower than the universities had received between 1945 and 1980, and was therefore viewed by them as a series of cuts. There was actually only one period of real cuts under Margaret Thatcher, during the very early years of her Government, when she cut the University Grants Council annual budget in real terms by 8 per cent. Because a significant part of the British academic science budget came from the infrastructural support to university science provided by the UGC, this did represent a real cut in academic science budgets over a two to three year period. But Mrs Thatcher was quite a conventional supporter of the state funding of science. The cut in the UGC budget was based on a comparative analysis which showed that student:staff ratios in Britain were lower than in any other country in the world but Holland. At a time when Britain was struggling financially, and was enjoying a GDP per capita of less than 60 per cent of those of our major trading partners (the USA, France and Germany, with Japan catching up fast), Mrs Thatcher found it absurd that we were funding our universities so generously. She cut their budgets. Interestingly, the Dutch government was cutting its higher education budgets at the same time and for similar reasons. The response of the British universities to these cuts was to compare Mrs Thatcher, to her disadvantage, to Hitler (literally so in *The Oxford Magazine*) and with other philistines. At the same time a group of British scientists created a prominent lobby group called Save British Science, which claimed dubiously that British science was in terrible decline because of Mrs Thatcher's cruel cuts and that the British economy would therefore enter into terminal collapse.

But the facts of British science under Thatcher are interesting because they demonstrate the effects of 'crowding out', and the power of purported experts to create false public impressions. Save British Science's big propaganda coup was to show that the share of scientific papers globally that was published by British scientists fell by 10 per cent during the 1970s. Decline! Quite how that was meant to be the responsibility of Mrs Thatcher (Prime Minister from 1979 to 1990) was never fully explained, but in the hysterical climate of the times many a distinguished professor was prepared to blame Margaret Thatcher for every unfortunate event that had assailed humanity since the expulsion of Adam and Eve from the Garden of Eden. The facts of the 10 per cent decline in Britain's share of world papers become even more puzzling when one notes that over the 1970s American, French and German science were also in decline. Was Margaret Thatcher responsible for those declines as well? No, of course not. The reality is that science amongst the developed nations grows absolutely (as judged by numbers of scientists, budgets and numbers of papers published) with a doubling time of about fifteen years. The rate of expansion of science, which has been linear in its inexorable growth since 1750, is astonishing and gave rise to the famous words of Derek da Sola Price that the statement that '80–90 per cent of all the scientists who have ever lived are alive today' has been true for every year since 1750.

The rate of scientific growth, however, amongst rapidly converging countries such as Japan, the other countries of the Pacific Rim and the countries of the Mediterranean rim including Greece, Italy and Spain is even greater, just as their GDPs per capita grow faster than those of the lead countries on which they are converging. During the 1970s, what we actually saw was an absolute growth in developed-country science (including Britain's) of about 50 per cent (i.e. very real indeed) but a growth in converging-country science of about 70 per cent. Britain's apparent decline of 10 per cent globally was only relative, not absolute, and merely reflected a most desirable growth of science outside the traditional scientific countries. Indeed it is astonishing that Britain, with 1 per cent of the world's population, publishes 9 per cent of the world's science.

Another extraordinary phenomenon of the Thatcher years was inadvertent demonstration of 'crowding out', the phenomenon by which the provision by government of a private good will cause its private provision to dry up. Economists have argued science to be a 'public good' because the fixed costs of producing scientific research are very high, the marginal costs almost zero (papers, patents and products can be easily read, plagiarized and copied). Consequently, it is argued, the private sector will 'under-provide' science because competitors will 'free-ride' since generators of new knowledge cannot capture all its benefits themselves. Yet when during the 1980s the Thatcher Government increased the funding for academic science at only about 30 per cent in real terms, that rate of increase fell below the natural rate of increase of approximately 50 per cent or more per decade that we have seen since 1750. The consequence was that the private funding for academic science doubled over that period to compensate.[2]

Industrial science also crowds out: when the OECD performed a wide multiple regression across its member states it found that: 'publicly performed R&D crowds out resources that could be alternatively used by the private sector, including private R&D'.[3]

Science may behave as a private, not a public good, primarily because it is a largely tacit good that, contrary to myth, is transferred only slowly, with difficulty and at great expense. When the economist Edwin Mansfield examined 48 products that during the 1970s had been copied by companies in the chemicals, drugs, electronics and machinery industries of New England, he found that the costs of copying were, on average, 65 per cent of the costs of original invention. Copying is expensive because each copier has to rediscover the tacit information embedded within the innovation. But copiers first have to discover that there is a discovery or patent or process or product to copy. As George Stigler showed, acquiring that by systematically reading the research papers and patents, attending the meetings, and sustaining the collaborations, is expensive. And as Rosenberg (1990), and Cohen and Levinthal (1989) have shown, companies have to provide their scientists with considerable freedom to research as they wish to allow them to sustain their tacit knowledge such that they can access others' science.[4] When those three costs are added (the cost of copying specific inventions, the costs of sustaining the tacit knowledge of a company's scientists and the costs of acquiring information about one's competitors) it can be seen that copying costs as much as innovation. It may be a myth that science is a public good that requires government subsidies.

Indeed, before 1940, 80 per cent of US scientific research was done in the private sector. The federal government funded only defence and some agricultural research, and they yielded few economic benefits. Yet by 1890 the US, already the richest country in the world in terms of GDP per capita and total factor productivity, was producing researchers of the quality of Edison and the Wright brothers in the absence of federal government support. Since 1940 the federal support for science has increased a thousandfold in real terms, but the US's long-term rates of economic and productivity growth have been unchanged.

Countries like the Soviet Union, India and Britain (under Harold Wilson's 'White Heat of the Technological Revolution') poured government money into science to no economic benefit at all. There is simply inadequate evidence that governments need to fund science. I believe that instead, they should lower taxes and leave research to the market and the great foundations.

But Mrs Thatcher herself was uninterested in such subtleties, impatient with suggestions that science was not a public good and did not need to be supplied publicly. She was herself a science graduate who had been educated at Oxford in chemistry during the Second World War, a time when faith in the government-funded science was never higher. She subscribed, as was then conventional, to Bacon's linear model, first formulated in 1605, which suggested that governments had to fund pure science to provide the applied science off which industry feeds to create wealth:

government-funded pure science → industrial-funded applied science →
economic growth

That model was contradicted by Adam Smith in his 1776 *Wealth of Nations*, where he showed that advances in both applied and pure science largely flowed out of industry, but this has been largely forgotten and Bacon's linear model prevails. The Russians won lots of Nobel Prizes and were the first to orbit the earth in Sputnik, but failed economically. Nobel Prizes bear no more causally on economic growth than do the gold medals at the Olympics that the East Germans specialized in.

As a Prime Minister who followed Bacon's linear model, Margaret Thatcher was surprisingly prescriptive, and she personally chaired the Committee on Science and Technology. In that role, she personally vetoed a £1 million MRC grant that had been passed by peer review to study the sexual practices in Britain as part of an anti-Aids campaign because she felt that the survey was meretricious and intrusive.

Equally, Mrs Thatcher took a personal interest in the human genome project, and helped ensure its early government funding. The irrelevance of that project's government funding was to be demonstrated by Craig Ventor who showed how the privately funded mapping of the human genome research was faster than the state's. But Mrs Thatcher prided herself as a scientist who could 'pick scientific winners' and, as noted, as early as 1979 she was anticipating and helping foster the upcoming IT revolution.

Margaret Thatcher was thus a surprisingly conventional Conservative in her treatment of science. She believed that the state should have an important input into the management and direction of higher education and research and she had a simplistic view of the relationship between academic science, economic growth and, indeed, national pride. She saw it as a government responsibility to the economy and to a nation's standing to promote the numbers of Nobel prizes.

Equally, she strengthened the government control of universities and their science. It was on her watch that the 1988 Higher Education Act was passed which greatly increased central government control of the universities by abolishing the University Grants Committee (a hands-off collection of academics who distributed the state's money with little state direction) and replacing it with the Higher Education Funding Councils which were staffed by civil servants and business people and which responded to government directions. That 1988 Act also abolished tenure for academics and introduced *dirigiste* practices adopted from commerce such as staff appraisals – practices of dubious applicability to universities. The Act also weakened scientific autonomy by forcing researchers to follow the *dirigiste* practices of the Research Assessment Exercises.

As she strengthened the *dirigisme* of the state in this manner, so Mrs Thatcher also determined that the state should maximize the commercial benefits of its science. She had been outraged by the failure of the MRC during the 1970s to patent monoclonal antibodies and she established a new regulatory framework to ensure that no such patent failure recurred – she wanted value for public money. Margaret Thatcher was, in short, a corporatist on Bismarckian lines. She believed in a strong state and in its strong direction of science and higher education.

Her legacy is thus mixed. The increased centralized direction of science and of higher education has been damaging to the academic spirit of free enquiry, which may be why some of the best universities in the world remain the independent American Ivy League colleges, not the state-run academies of Britain, France, Germany or Japan. On the other hand, Mrs Thatcher did inaugurate a new era of financial responsibility within the universities. It was Margaret Thatcher, for example, who insisted that foreign students pay full fees, and though this initiative was greeted with dismay by the British universities at the time, her judgement proved to be correct, and after a transient drop in foreign student numbers those numbers have doubled and doubled again, and they now supply a very significant source of income to British universities.

Unfortunately, though, the regulatory stranglehold that she and her Secretary of State for Education, Kenneth Baker, established in 1988 has not allowed the British universities yet to translate their increased financial autonomy from the state into greater administrative autonomy on the American Ivy League model. The top-up fee initiative of Tony Blair's Government will eventually see much greater financial autonomy for British universities, who will demand greater administrative autonomy. The London School of Economics, for example, is funded largely autonomously because most of its students come from outside the EU and they pay full fees. When, during the early 2000s, the LSE found the inspections of the Quality Assurance Agency to be over-prescriptive and to imperil, in the LSE's own words, its academic freedom, the LSE threatened to leave the public sector. Consequently the CEO of the QAA resigned and the QAA lightened its touch. Financial autonomy translates into academic autonomy, and it was Margaret Thatcher who inaugurated the new era of academic financial autonomy.

Mrs Thatcher applauded with words the independent sector in higher education, but in practice was more comfortable with a large state-funded and, of course, very impressive institution. Margaret Thatcher was a Good Thing for British science and higher education because by her acts she helped render the sectors more commercial and more financially autonomous. She was a Bad Thing in that she did not question the simplistic assumption that science and higher education are public goods, and she thus imposed too great a state control over them. But in the long term the greater financial autonomies she introduced will eventually work to render them more autonomous in their governance. She was, therefore, taken overall, Quite a Good Thing.

Notes

1   www.margaretthatcher.org/Speeches. This paragraph is co-authored with Subroto Roy.

2   See T. Kealey, *The Economic Laws of Scientific Research* (Macmillan Press, 1996), Chapter 11. J. Irvine *et al.* (1985) 'Charting the Decline of British Science' *Nature*, 316: 587–90. D. da S. Price *Little Science, Big Science* (Columbia University Press, 1963). T. Kealey (1991) 'Government Funded Science is a Consumer Good Not a Producer Good: A Commentary on the Scientometrics of Irvine and Martin', *Scientometrics*, 20: 369–94. J. Bray (1989) *Science for the Citizen* (London: Labour Party); Association of University Teachers (1989) *The Case for Increased Investment in our Universities* (London: Association of University Teachers).

3   OECD (2003) *The Sources of Economic Growth in OECD Countries*, p. 84.
4   E. Mansfield *et al.* (1981) 'Imitation Costs and Patents: An Empirical Study', *Economic Journal*, 91: 907–18. G. J. Stigler (1961) 'The Economics of Information', *Journal of Political Economy*, 64: 213–25. N. Rosenberg (1990) 'Why Do Firms Do Basic Research With Their Own Money?', *Research Policy*, 19: 165–74. W. M. Cohen and D. A. Levinthal (1989) 'Innovation and Learning: The Two Faces of R&D', *Economic Journal*, 99: 569–96.

10 Creating alternatives to the NHS

David Marsland

Doctors and nurses are highly regarded, and quite properly so. Their work in any human society is widely seen as immeasurably valuable. Hospitals and clinics in which they work are viewed by everyone as crucial local and national institutions. The mission of healthcare – curing illness, relieving pain, repairing injury, preventing disease and saving lives – justifiably ranks close to the top of any nation's priorities.

Unfortunately, all these positive popular sentiments have been in Britain unthinkingly and uncritically invested since 1948 in the National Health Service. A particular, concrete social organization – established more than fifty years ago in a specific and peculiar historical context, a fossilized remnant of the post-War welfare settlement – has been (illegitimately) endowed with the high public reputation which properly belongs to the healthcare professions, to great hospitals and successful clinics, and to the medical scientists who advance the knowledge on which effective healthcare relies.

This displacement of positive feeling from healthcare institutions and the long-established values and skills of medicine onto the recent, historically accidental and politically contingent organizational format of the NHS is at once confusing and damaging. It inhibits radical criticism of the NHS. It provides a cloak of ideological defence for the most reactionary elements in the NHS workforce. It inoculates the popular mind against awareness of the grave and growing deficiencies of the NHS. It blinds our political leaders to the fact that healthcare in the United Kingdom is as modestly effective as it is not *because* of the NHS, but *despite* it.

Aneurin Bevan won a titanic struggle against the medical profession, the Conservative Party and much of the media to establish the National Health Service in 1948. By means of a single legislative decision the complex mixed-economy of the established healthcare system was transmuted into a massive unitary organization directed by Whitehall. Ownership and control of the whole healthcare system became at the stroke of a pen a socialized government monopoly. Independent, charitable, voluntary and municipal hospitals, general and specialized, large and small, first-class and indifferent in quality, all of them were swallowed up. Hundreds of thousands of doctors in every medical specialty, nurses, ancillary workers and others were transferred en bloc to the state's payroll. A massive and immensely valuable estate of buildings, plant and land fell at little cost into the state's outstretched hands. Little wonder if socialists even of the extreme left acclaimed the establishment of the NHS as a glorious stride on the journey towards their secular Jerusalem.

In Bevan, the Labour Government had an eloquent spokesman and a tough negotiator. And it was a plausible pitch. He highlighted the grossly inadequate healthcare available to the poor, the lack of investment in the War years and earlier, the patchy variability of provision across the country, the supposedly mercenary motivations of private doctors and the complete lack of national strategy and planning. Looking to the future, he promised free healthcare for everyone, new hospitals, more doctors and nurses, and planned, lifelong care. In short, free dentures and spectacles today – immortality tomorrow.

The population, many Conservative supporters among them, believed him. The Opposition, at first reluctantly and soon enthusiastically, accepted the NHS as a *fait accompli*. Even the media began to recognize that criticism of the new service was counter-productive.

Yet in fact the National Health Service Act reproduced, even exaggerated, in the sphere of healthcare the error made in education almost a century earlier by the Forster Act of 1870. In each case, inadequacies of provision for a small minority were used as a justification for wholesale nationalization – and thus in the longer term gravely damaged provision made for the whole population.

For, like all nationalized industries, the NHS suffered and continues to suffer from the several inevitable faults of state monopoly: bureaucracy, giantism, planning mania, and inhumanity. The utopian dream which underlay the foundation of the NHS was subjected from the start to the harsh challenge of these realities. From its inception the monopolistic position of the NHS prevented learning from competition and from experience, and so did not attend better than merely adequately to patients' needs and concerns. Its bureaucratic structure has consistently prevented it from operating with the adaptable flexibility and attention to varied and changing needs and concerns which we take for granted from service-providers in the private sector. Its colossal scale inhibits innovation and encourages depersonalized routinization. The commitment of its senior managers to centralized planning, and the entrapment of managers at all levels within its quasi-Soviet toils, stands in the way of local and individual initiative and enterprise, and limits genuine concern with the reactions of patients and families.

Worst of all, dogmatic adherence in the NHS, as a matter of foundational principle, to the concept of generalized universalism contradicts the more fundamental principles of genuine charity – which require recognition of individuality, agency and responsibility. In consequence the NHS has become more and more inhuman and thus more and more ineffective.

Throughout the years 1948–79 there were some significant changes in the structure of the NHS, particularly towards the close of the period. During the same period there were also improvements – in healthcare facilities, in quality of care, in medical science (especially pharmaceuticals) and even, to a degree, in efficiency. However, the same period saw incomparably more substantial advances in standards of living, in the quality of private sector services, and consequently in the ambition of public expectations. By comparison, the NHS was dropping behind. Before the 1970s were out, the crowning glory of the British welfare state, as it had seemed in 1948, was more than a little tarnished.

Moreover, the changes in organization introduced from time to time, even including the most substantial changes initiated by the Conservative Government in the early 1970s, achieved little more than administrative restructuring. These were enough to disturb the work patterns of healthcare professionals somewhat, but did little to counter the self-destructive centripetal trend inherent in nationalized systems. This is evident from the admitted aims spelled out in the 1973 NHS Act – unification of health services under Regional Health Authorities, better coordination of health services with local authority services, and modernized management.

Christopher Ham has said of these reforms 'after almost twenty-six years the NHS underwent a major organizational change' (Ham, 1992, p. 27). Perhaps – but the direction of the change thus initiated was towards yet further and tighter centralization under stricter and ever less-forgiving state control. This is less like oil spread on troubled waters than petrol flung with cavalier abandon on the flames.

But one thing at least did change very substantially during this period: the scale of public expenditure devoted to the NHS. Lord Beveridge and other early supporters of socialized medicine had claimed naïvely and absurdly that expenditure would actually decrease as the population got healthier with the benefit of modernized NHS provision. The prediction went wildly wrong from the start. In defiance of its own principles, the Labour Government had to introduce prescription charges within just a few years of the establishment of the 'free' NHS. Then in 1953 the Guillebaud Committee was set up to consider what were already by now acknowledged as worrying increases in healthcare costs. Hemmed in by research from such avid supporters of socialized medicine as

Richard Titmuss and Brian Abel-Smith, Guillebaud produced an over-sanguine report suggesting that 'there was no evidence of extravagance or inefficiency in the NHS' (Ham, 1992, p. 18). Yet between 1949 and 1979 NHS expenditure increased from a meagre £437 million to a massive £9283 million – in real terms an increase of more than 300 per cent (Office of Health Economics, 1989). As a proportion of GDP this is almost a doubling. It is a very substantial increase in real terms every year for over three decades, most of it going to pay for the salaries of a continuously (and haphazardly) growing, poorly organized, low-productivity workforce.

By 1979 the NHS we were all supposed to be so proud of, the Labour Party's universal free utopia, was recognized by increasing numbers of academics, politicians, journalists, and not least patients and their families, as seriously flawed. Despite massive continuing 'investment', so-called, the NHS model of healthcare was comparing badly both with the market-plus-insurance-plus-targeted-assistance model of the USA, and with continental approaches based on genuine insurance disciplined by user charges unapologetically applied rather than general taxation.

Nor was the apparent superiority of these alternative models limited to their more realistic financial structure. They also offered, by contrast with the National Health Service's state monopoly, a wide variety of competing suppliers, public and private, with competitive emulation fuelling dynamic improvements in service quality. Moreover, as the IMF bailiffs were called in to sort out the Labour Government's public expenditure crisis in 1976, industrial action brought Britain's generalized ungovernability into the heart of the NHS. It was evident that radical reform was required.

However, while the need for reform was pressing, it was not immediately answered. Until 1987 the Thatcher Governments were largely preoccupied with salvaging and restructuring the economy, with dealing with the trade unions, with defending British interests, territory and people against invasion by armed force, and with responding to the destructive challenge of the miners' strike. There was little enough time or energy left over for radical, large-scale reform of welfare.

However, even these early achievements made an indispensable contribution to that end. Without the active shake-out of the economy, without the liberalization of capital markets, without sweeping tax-cuts, without wholesale privatization, and without the taming of the trade unions, the successful, modernized, enterprise economy today would have been impossible. Without these economic achievements, radical reform of welfare would have been inconceivable. At best we would have had – as we did not have – merely savage cuts in public expenditure, social division, and no welfare reform at all. The triumph of Margaret Thatcher in transforming a near-bankrupt economy into a thriving enterprise culture should not be underestimated.

However, economic change is not in itself enough. On those twin pillars of the welfare state, the National Health Service and state education, the government moved with caution. The Prime Minister realized only too well how bitterly the Opposition would criticize any radical reform which the media could be persuaded to interpret as an attack on the welfare state.

Nonetheless, careful analysis and thorough preparations were made for reform on both fronts. Legislation and implementation came as late as 1988 and 1989, stretching beyond the Thatcher Governments in both cases, namely the Education Reform Act 1988 and NHS and Community Care Act 1990. In both cases the thrust of reform was similar – enhanced attention to the consumer's role, introduction of competition, devolution of management to local operating levels, and tough central frameworking. It has been argued that Mrs Thatcher was here too cautious and, even worse, too centralizing. I suspect her political judgement was sound – as reactions even within the Cabinet to the radical proposals of the 1982 CPRS report and the later debacle over the Community Charge demonstrated. Neither a voucher system for education nor privatized healthcare supplying free delivery were (or are even now) politically feasible. And in the absence of real markets, central monitoring was essential if the vested interests of teachers, doctors and nurses were to be resisted successfully. Moreover, these two great reforms – driven through against shrill resistance in the late 1980s and the 1990s – have provided, despite cosmetic changes under Labour since 1997, an essential basis for Tony Blair's attempts at modernization since 2001. On education and healthcare it has to be concluded that Margaret Thatcher's achievements in challenging and permanently subverting the orthodoxy of welfare state thinking were considerable.

In healthcare, education and social services, the quasi-market, mixed economy model of 1987 – the year which David Willetts has called the 'annus mirabilis' of Conservative social policy – was fully implemented in the face of powerful resistance by the welfare workforce and established social policy experts. On all three of these major fronts of the welfare state – with housing also added – a coherent national framework was established incorporating both local competitive autonomy and central government frameworking, standard-setting and regulation. Purchasing and providing partners were defined, where necessary created, and linked by competition and contract. The concept of quality was taken over from its industrial and business origins, and implemented toughly with a view to consumer satisfaction.

Now, as Timmins says of the original 1987 proposals from which the reforms sprang, they could serve either as a springboard for radical denationalization or to the contrary as a trigger for consumers to cling to state welfare and demand ever higher standards. While this is certainly true, it also has to be acknowledged that these reforms:

1. Represent a fundamental challenge and a serious alternative to the pre-1979 paternalistic, monolithic welfare state.
2. Are so patently an improvement on what went before that no government of whatever party would reverse them or change them better than partially.

3. Keep alive the possibility of denationalization, and provide a framework through which this could be accomplished.
4. Take reform about as far as is for the time being politically feasible, with next steps awaiting economic stringency, popular dissatisfaction with standards provided in the state sector by comparison with the market sphere, or recognition of the damaging effects of state welfare.

On the specifics of healthcare reform by Conservative governments between 1979 and 1997, preparation was deliberate and careful. This included a Ministerial Review of the National Health Service and the White Papers *Working for patients* and *Health of the Nation*. The primary legislative expression of reform was the NHS and Community Care Act of 1990. Implementation of reform was put in the hands of Kenneth Clarke who pursued it carefully, cautiously and where necessary ruthlessly – in the face of widespread resistance.

Much of this resistance was irrational, since, apart from token tax rebates for the over-60s for private healthcare, there was no trace of the malign intention of privatizing healthcare and thus abandoning the NHS which the Opposition alleged.

The key reforms were as follows:

• Establishment of NHS Hospital Trusts, allowing major hospitals to become self-governing. Privatization was explicitly excluded and local coverage of essential tasks was guaranteed. The Trusts were to be the key providers – answerable in an internal quasi-market to the purchasing requirements of their consumers.

• The structure of the Health Authorities was changed fundamentally, with smaller, more streamlined Authorities serving as crucial agents of purchasing and monitoring.

• Established methods of resource allocation – widely regarded as antiquated, over-complex and ritualistically formulaic – were scrapped, and replaced with simpler methods and an internal market pushing funding towards patients and their needs. Real attention to costs was required for the first time since 1948.

- The quality of management throughout the NHS was high-lighted, modernized and strengthened. A balance was required between localized initiative and overall accountability.
- The number of consultants was significantly increased, com-bined with strengthened medical audit.
- The role of general practitioners was acknowledged, empha-sized and enhanced. Larger practices to have their own budgets, with discretion to spend it on their patients' behalf. At the same time, the need for careful attention to costs and savings was emphasized.
- The role of patients as consumers was emphasized, with requirements in relation to all providers for appointment systems, improved waiting rooms and family facilities, and better complaints procedures.
- Tax relief on private healthcare insurance for the over-60s was introduced, and collaborative partnerships between the NHS and the independent sector were encouraged.

In the context of the first thirty static and declining years of the NHS, these reforms were quite radical. But they were hardly rev-olutionary. Indeed, while they opened up the internal structure of the NHS considerably, they seem to have somewhat strength-ened central government control of healthcare overall. Patients newly recognized as consumers, and structural elements of NHS organizational machinery empowered for the first time to serve dynamically as purchasers and providers in a market situation were both, nonetheless, contained and protected within a fundamentally unchanged NHS framework. Without real privatization, it could hardly be otherwise if costs were not to be driven through the roof.

As 1997 approached, the Conservative reforms – sensibly modified where practical problems required it, ruthlessly pushed through where resistance was merely ideological – seemed to be bedding down quite well. Staff adapted to market concepts, new management styles, attention to consumers, and rapidly changing demands remarkably well. Alas, the Labour Party decided to seize opportunistically on an entirely fictitious threat to privatize the NHS which they attributed, quite contrary to the evidence, to the Government. A key plank in Labour's election campaign was that they would 'save the NHS'. The first serious attempt at reform of the National Health Service since its inception was about to be cut off in its prime.

After the 1997 election, Mr Blair and his ministers behaved, up to a point, as if they believed their own propaganda about the supposed Conservative threat to the National Health Service. To redeem their electoral promise to 'save the NHS', a decidedly Old Labour Secretary of State for Health was appointed, tax rebates were cancelled, the structure of health authorities and Trusts was made bureaucratic again, and flows of resources began once more to respond to central command rather than to consumer needs mediated by purchasing agents with teeth.

However, the pre-1979 structures were not restored. The purchaser–provider contract relationship was not outlawed or fully replaced. There was no let-up in central pressure on local health services to pay careful attention to the minimization of costs and the modernization of management, and to construe patients as consumers. Indeed, hospitals, doctors and healthcare managers have been subjected ever since 1997 to an ever-expanding flood of new initiatives, new targets and new monitoring controls.

But neither promises nor prodding had much effect. Scandals and patent inefficiencies proliferated as never before, as right and left in Parliament, in the media and academia conspired in exposure and condemnation of the Government's failure with healthcare. When this situation eventually became too much to spin aside, the Government reverted to tax-and-spend, with the announcement of truly massive expansion in expenditure on the NHS up to 2007 – an increase of 7.1 per cent per annum above inflation, to be paid for from increased National Insurance contributions. With the aim of trumping average European expenditure on healthcare, NHS costs were targeted to rise to above £100 billion every year before the end of the decade (see DoH 2000).

While this healthcare bonanza was greeted on the left with acclaim, and by other supporters of the NHS with relief, it was immediately criticized by neutral commentators as certain to require further tax increases in the long run – and in any case unlikely to produce the desired improvements in NHS performance. Moreover, Mr Blair insisted that 'investment', as it was optimistically if less than accurately called, had to be balanced by 'reform'.

The introduction of Foundation Hospitals with considerably enhanced managerial and financial autonomy was pushed through successfully – in the face of widespread opposition in Parliament and in the Labour Party, and at the very real risk of a damaging Parliamentary defeat. Furthermore, Primary Care Trusts were established and strengthened as crucial purchasing agencies, with some at least of the dynamic power of the Conservative arrangements earlier dismantled. As a further stimulus to modernization, bureaucratic targets were somewhat reduced, and at every turn the independent sector was lauded and wherever feasible utilized.

By 2004 the results of this flurry of somewhat incoherent activity was widespread confusion, with the left nervous about possible privatization, the right – more realistically – concerned about the dangers of modernized corporatism, and most people outside New Labour's coterie ranks desperately anxious about the huge costs involved and unconvinced about the likelihood of any real change in healthcare efficiency.

At the time of writing in 2004, both major parties are emphasizing the importance of 'choice' for patients and clients. Neither is at all clear about its views of optimal structures, of feasible funding levels, or of the proper balance between local professional autonomy and centralized managerial control. The manifestly confused and self-contradictory state of play in the Government's approach to healthcare is described in the annual official record of the social policy establishment; Allsop and Baggott (2004, p. 29) say 'It is possible to interpret the policies that have developed as having elements of both modernization and marketization. "Modernization" can be seen as an attempt to shift the political economy of the National Health Service from a centralized command and control model, with its associated corporate politics, towards the delivery of health services through a series of separate local, independently managed components. The efficient and effective use of resources in this developed NHS is to be achieved by, on the one hand, centralized controls that hold local providers accountable for achieving particular outcomes, and on the other, by the manipulation of both demand and supply side factors to alter the behaviour of those who consume and those who provide health care.

'Underlying Labour's policies is therefore a recognition of the power of "market" forces. Politically "modernization" is driven through enhancing and harnessing the powers of healthcare users as individuals wishing to access good quality healthcare, while at the same time curbing the potential monopoly powers of those who provide that healthcare through new employment contracts and changes in the division of healthcare tasks.'

One does not need to follow Allsop and Baggott to their predictable conclusion that modernization is fine while marketization is anathema, to recognize in their description that the Government has arrived at a developmental cul-de-sac in the evolution of the NHS. Either genuine reform which would fundamentally challenge the founding principles of the NHS has to be entered upon; or the inefficiency, poor quality and extravagant costs of British healthcare will continue to worsen, with systemic collapse likely before long.

Between 1979 and 1997 Conservative governments, motivated by Margaret Thatcher's commitment to freedom and antipathy to state welfare, pushed attempts at reforming the NHS hard, and made remarkable progress. They were foiled by electoral defeat and more fundamentally by their unwillingness to grasp the nettle of denationalization. Since 1997 the Government, guided by Tony Blair's New Labour recognition that the established collectivist welfare system is outmoded and inefficient, has reached around – courageously but increasingly desperately – for some new magic ingredient which might cure the healthcare malaise. This too has proved a failure – and for the same reason as Conservative attempts at reform failed earlier. Neither of the major political parties is willing to acknowledge that nationalized healthcare may be finished and that only denationalization can open up a route towards progress.

There are still some avenues open for further reform within the established system. Given the extreme political difficulty – to put it rather mildly – of winning parliamentary and public support for denationalization, these half-measures seem likely to be essayed in the short term. For example, by making individual patients fundholders, the promise of choice and consumer power could be given practical effect (see Spiers 2003). Instead of merely ritual talk about choice, Spiers' radical proposals would genuinely empower patients, require of them responsibility and mature autonomy in respect of their own healthcare, and stimulate quality improvements by a more diversified and consumer-driven set of providers.

Or again the valuable efforts of the independent sector could be more closely coordinated with the NHS and more comprehensively incorporated into its work nationwide. If prejudices in policy-making circles and among the medical establishment could be tempered somewhat, the independent sector offers a ready-made public–private partnership which would enhance the capacity and the quality of NHS provision immeasurably. Or, thirdly among these possible partial-reform measures, charges might be levied for elements of healthcare provision. Modest fees to be paid for the hotel aspect of hospital care, for consultations with GPs and for use of medical equipment would restrain excess demand and provide significant revenues for financing core healthcare services.

However, none of these is likely to answer the grave problems of nationalized healthcare. Only denationalization may suffice. Reform of the healthcare supply-side is relatively straightforward. All that is required is a further instalment of privatization – the biggest programme of privatization of them all. Provider-agencies, hospitals, clinics, practices, advice centres, laboratories – the whole vast machinery of healthcare – should be sold off. The prospective purchasers would include insurance companies, healthcare businesses, local managers, independent practitioners, charitable agencies, and trade unions. Notwithstanding Barr's influential contrary arguments (1998), a diversified, competitive healthcare industry would be more efficient, more cost-effective, more consumer-oriented and more innovative than the NHS can ever manage.

The demand side is more difficult. Five decades of 'free' healthcare have persuaded much of the population that doctors and nurses grow on trees gratis and that medicines can be picked up for nothing under stones. Denationalization will be feasible only if the genuinely poor, especially among pensioners, are protected in the first instance against full healthcare costs. For the majority, generous tax rebates should ensure voluntary involvement in insurance and other independent alternatives to state provision on a large scale. Once initiated, an independent self-care system would grow rapidly as its benefits became apparent. Within a decade, the NHS – retitled as the Healthcare Benefits Unit and located within the Department of Social Security – would be a small organization with a modest and reducing budget, serving progressively fewer people.

Radical reform along these lines is entirely feasible in medical, administrative and financial terms. The weak link is political. If genuine reform of healthcare – and of the welfare state more broadly – is to be accomplished, we shall need confident, visionary leadership such as Margaret Thatcher provided for the heroic first wave of denationalization in the 1980s. The NHS has been from the start a utopian dream. It should be replaced before it collapses entirely by a healthcare system founded on more sensible assumptions about human nature, economic realities and organizational functioning, a healthcare system built unapologetically on self-reliance, responsibility, choice and competition.[1]

Notes

A bibliography for further reference is as follows: N. Timmins, *The Five Giants: a biography of the Welfare State* (London: HarperCollins, 2001); E. G. West, *Education and the State* (London: Institute of Economic Affairs, 1965); J. Allsop and R. Baggott, 'The NHS in England: from modernization to marketisation?' in N. Ellison *et al.*, *Social Policy Review 16: analysis and debate in social policy* (London: Policy Press for the Social Policy Association, 2004); N. Barr, *The Economics of the Welfare State* (Oxford: Oxford University Press, 1998); J. Campbell, *Nye Bevan: a biography* (London: Hodder and Stoughton, 1987); DoH, *The NHS Plan* 2000 (Cmd 4818, London: The Stationery Office); Guillebaud Committee (1956 Report of the Committee of Enquiry into the Cost of the National Health Service (Cmd 9663, HMSO); Christopher Ham, *Health Policy in Britain: the politics and organisation of the National Health Service* (Basingstoke: Macmillan, 3rd edition, 1992); D. Marsland, *Welfare or Welfare State?* (Basingstoke: Macmillan, 1996); *Not Cancelled – Postponed: a revolution in healthcare* (Health Business Summary, Vol. 13, No. 1, pp. 4–9, 1996; D. Marsland and E. Mathura, *Public Service Plus: the role of the independent sector in health care* (Health Summary, Vol. 13, No. 11, pp. 8–12, 1996; *Compendium of Health Statistics* (London: OHE, 7th edition, 1989); J. Spiers, *Patients, Power and Responsibility: the first principles of consumer-driven reform* (Abingdon: Radcliffe Medical Press, 2003); M. Thatcher, *The Downing Street Years* (London: HarperCollins, 1993).

11 Thatcher's Conservatism: a hypothesis

Norman Barry

Margaret Thatcher is unique in modern politics in having a doctrine named after her. Even socialist leaders have not had ideologies attached to their names; while conservatives traditionally claimed political virtue in not being associated with an integrated set of ideas from which one can read off a response to a policy issue. Some traditional conservatives were always sceptical of her policies precisely because they seemed to be inspired by laissez-faire theorists, some of whom, like F. A. Hayek, were foreign in origin. Yet, though Thatcherism was not a political or economic theory like Marxism or classical liberalism, it was inspired by a set of cogent ideas.

Just what this amounted to may be understood by distinguishing two types of conservatism: what I have elsewhere called *dispositional* and *substantive*.[1] Dispositional conservatives have a reverence for the past that excludes any rational evaluation of its features; it is to be valued merely because it provides us with a storehouse of lessons which we can apply to contemporary problems. These at the most amount to practices worth preserving. Thus *apparatchiks* of the Communist Party who resisted the revolutionary changes in Eastern Europe were called conservative, as are Islamic fundamentalists.

But it is doubtful if any classic British conservative has adhered consistently to an anti-rational approach. Even the much revered Edmund Burke had a clear laissez-faire economic ideology.[2] His pamphlet, *Thoughts and Details on Scarcity*, was an extreme celebration on the mechanics of market society that matched any-thing produced by Adam Smith. It was his recognition of the power of economic laws and an acknowledgement of the folly of governments attempting to resist their ineluctable operation that makes him a market theorist.[3] Although their ideas may be derived from the past they do embody certain values and principles. They are adopted and preserved for a *reason*. And they might even be suitable for export, as the English common law was imposed on the former Empire, and preserved by many independent coun-tries. British conservatism may never have been ideologically committed to the free market but it has always been anxious to maintain those economic institutions that have been successful; since the exchange system is intimately bound up with freedom and property even a strident commitment to it would not be unconservative.

By my definition, Margaret Thatcher's conservatism is mainly of the substantive type while several of her adversaries were dis-positional conservatives who believed that certain changes in twentieth-century Britain, including a modest socialism, were unalterable and constituted a 'consensus' which it would be folly to disturb. They had become accustomed to a 'middle way' between capitalism and socialism. The latter could only be moder-ated and it would be foolish to try to turn back an irrevocable tide. But Thatcher had other ideas; although these did not constitute a fully-fledged theory, they revealed an attitude of mind that provided her with appropriate responses to the contingencies of the moment and sensible strategies for the future. Though this had roots in the past, it is important to see it was as much a response to the *errors* of the immediate past as it was a celebration of the virtues of tradition. For Thatcherism was born of one overwhelming fact: the decline of Britain in the post-War years. When the Thatcher Government took office in 1979, inflation was approaching 20 per cent, the public sector was inexorably expanding, welfare had become a way of life for an increasing number, strikes were perva-sive, trade unions were the unofficial government, unemployment was rising, growth falling and the country was labelled the sick man of Europe. Thatcherian conservatives blamed the complaisant acceptance of the reforms of the Attlee Government which had *de facto* socialized the country with extensive nationalization, the creation of a vastly extended welfare state whose insurance-based principles were giving way to tax-funding and what was left of the private sector was subject to Keynesian demand management policies. The future promised more of the same. Some conservatives under the influence of the 'middle way' were active promoters of the post-War consensus. No Conservative (except Enoch Powell) had seriously challenged the prevailing paradigm. Edward Heath's Government in 1970 initially had a free market agenda but quickly retreated once unemployment rose above 500,000 and big companies were threatened with bankruptcy. It passed the Industry Act of 1972 which made economic intervention easy and was used extensively by Labour from 1974–79. Unusually, the Tories were badly in need of a doctrine. Self-seeking interest groups in public life prevented the emergence of a genuine common good. The consensus even at its best involved squalid deals between big business, big unions and big government.

Thatcherism was more than economics: it was a revival of what Shirley Robin Letwin identified as the 'vigorous virtues': those propensities of independence, self-confidence and initiative which had led to industrial success and the building of a benign empire.[4] They had been all but emasculated by decades of economic mismanagement and seductive but debilitating 'welfare'. By 1979 Britain had become a nation of dependants who were eager to look towards the state for solutions to all problems, economic, industrial and personal. The permissive society of the 1960s had not so much expanded liberty as relieved persons of real responsibility for action.

An 'economic determinist conservative' like myself maintains these problems can be handled with tools of microeconomics but that we have first to examine the orthodoxies of economic policy and Thatcher's alternative 'monetarist' diagnosis for the malaise of the 1970s. But monetarism was insufficient to solve the problem of poor economic performance. And there was also the relation between the government deficit and increase in the money supply, which became important in Thatcher's first term. By itself monetarism has little to do with the laissez-faire; a heavily interventionist government might adhere strictly to the new quantity theory of money.

The first goal of the 1979 Government was to defeat inflation. It was imperative the deficit be reduced. And the 1981 budget, which raised taxes for this purpose, provoked the ire of the members of the academic economics establishment, 364 of whom published a letter in *The Times* on 30 March 1981.[5] The government targeted a broad definition of money (M3) and gradually reduced inflation to less than 5 per cent. Here though we come to the first difficulty in Thatcherian economics, which had serious consequences for the 'doctrine'. Nigel Lawson abandoned the broad money target and instead tracked the Deutschmark. This resulted in the re-emergence of inflation by 1988 back at 10 per cent, and Thatcherian economics were in disarray. Although she publicly defended her Chancellor, Thatcher was not happy and appointed her own economic adviser, Alan Walters. There will be endless debates about the whole episode which led to the resignation of both Lawson and Walters. Thatcher's economics were only partially successful but they did at least end one illusion: that government could determine output, employment and other substantive economic matters by monetary and fiscal measures. Her economic adviser said she, not an economist, had the 'instincts' of an economist.

Economics was a necessary prelude to the Thatcher revolution. Unlike her predecessors, she wanted to roll back the state, encourage private initiative and restore faith in capitalism. She did not think the mistakes of forty years were irreversible and rejected the view that the role of government is 'the orderly management of decline'. At the forefront of her ideas was the belief in the value of freedom, not just as the necessary instrument for the achievement of efficiency but also for the development of the personality and the promotion of independence. Unlike 'liberals' as that term is used in America, she believed in the unity of liberty: it could not be divided into civil and economic liberty with the former ranked higher. As she well knew, if that is done economic freedom will be lost. It was no abstract concept but one firmly rooted in the British individualist tradition of common law and property. In a speech in Melbourne in 1976 she specifically rebuked the then Labour Government for its 'imperceptible' inroads into this conception.[6] At the same time she denied the validity of the burgeoning idea that there was something called 'collective liberty', apparently exemplified by the common consumption of public services. And in the same year as the Melbourne speech, when speaking in Zurich, she linked economic freedom with morality: it is derived from choice and personal responsibility for action. Successive post-War governments through extensive regulation, excessive taxation and unnecessary welfare were producing a nation of dependants. There are the socialists 'who consider they know what is good for people and those (conservatives) who think the people know best . . .'[7] Against the dispositional conservatives in her own party, who included such prominent figures as James Prior and Ian Gilmour, she was convinced that the clock could be turned back: there was nothing inevitable about socialism.

But to illustrate her conservatism rather than her classical liberalism, she showed no fear of the state in its legitimate role. There was always likely to be a conflict between liberty and order and a strong state is necessary for the preservation of *ordered* liberty, in which human action could be predicted and legitimate expectations are honoured. The enforcement of the law against violent strikers was what she had in mind: 'In our party we do not ask for a feeble state. On the contrary, we need a strong state to preserve both liberty and order, to prevent liberty from crumbling and to keep order hardening into despotism.'[8] It was not therefore the extent of state action that concerned her but its *character*.

But the state at her time was doing the wrong things so the major part of her strategy was to reduce it to its appropriate role. A privatization programme became imperative, not just for efficiency but for liberty; though its efficiency properties became crucial in its success. Although it was not part of her programme in 1979, the Thatcherians quickly realized the value of privatization. The return on capital was significantly less in the public sector than in the private and when they took office they faced a deficit of £4 billion in the nationalized industries: Thatcher was anxious to dismantle them. So in the early 1980s British Telecom and British Airways were sold off to the public and this established a pattern that was to be imitated throughout the world. It was a big step in her dream to create a property-owning democracy. If people had a vested interest in society they would be less likely to participate in the destructive action that had occurred throughout the 1970s.

Most significant was the selling off of council houses. They were not sold off at market prices but residents were given significant reductions for the time they had spent in the properties. This indicated that the goal was not strictly economic efficiency but to spread property widely and make individuals independent of local housing authorities and become self-reliant. This was an outstanding success and by the time the programme had been completed the proportion of people in private occupation had shifted upwards from 25 per cent to well over 50 per cent.

A major element in the attempt to return economic power to the people was tax cuts. Lawson was an outstanding tax chancellor. When the conservatives took office in 1979 the highest rate of tax was 83 per cent, fully consistent with Denis Healey's claim to punish 'the rich until the pips squeaked'. This was ruinous policy: the rich left the country, avoided the tax or stopped working. It was also an affront to Thatcher's idea of justice and, anyway, the money would be more productive if left in private hands. The top rate of tax was reduced to 40 per cent and the lower to 23 per cent with no loss in revenue to the Exchequer. Furthermore, through the creation of Personal Equity Plans (PEPS), tax-exempt shareholdings, the public got used to the idea of share ownership. It was part of her goal to democratize capitalism and make it as familiar to people as house ownership.

If any were responsible for destroying the post-War consensus it was the trade unions. Unlike any other European country Britain had a union problem throughout most of the twentieth century. It wasn't just that the unions were socialist, in fact for much of the period right-wing union leaders used the block vote at Labour Party conferences to forestall extremist resolutions. The problem was that they were a powerful interest group that could and did wreck consensus strategies, for example, prices and incomes policies. They were entirely self-interested but as Thatcher realized, self-interest in the private market leads to social harmony but in the industrial sphere, with monopoly unions, it produced permanent confrontation.

Since the Trade Disputes Act of 1906 unions were immune from the tort of inducement to breach contract, they used intimidation to persuade workers to join strikes and had developed the closed shop to keep out non-union members. Of course, economic research has demonstrated that these privileges did not advance the interests of the workers as a whole but they did enable powerful unions to divert income from the productive to the unproductive. They also gave them an unconstitutional role in government. They had been disruptive of both Labour and Conservative governments. Harold Wilson had tried but failed to reform them with *In Place of Strife* (1967) and Ted Heath had no better luck with his Industrial Relations Act (1971). Throughout the 1970s the country had been held to ransom by unions which were above the rule of law. And the Labour governments of 1974–79 substantially increased their powers. Secondary disputes, those that had no connection with the original conflict, were effectively legalized and 'flying pickets' roamed the country looking for trouble. It was worse for Labour who required union cooperation in their feeble attempts to control inflation without the unemployment that would have temporarily been created by a strict monetary policy. Matters came to a head in the 'Winter of

Discontent' (1978–79) when the Ford workers broke through the 4 per cent limit on wages to be quickly followed by others. Elementary social science tells us that it is impossible for large numbers voluntarily to pursue the 'common good' when so much can be gained by defection from the deal. Then, of course, they all defect and chaos results.

When Thatcher came into office she knew the unions had to be defeated, but how? Instead of trying a comprehensive reform, as had Wilson and Heath, she approached the matter almost incrementally. She whittled away at their powers bit by bit until the overall result was their total defeat. Four important statutes were passed, the Employment Acts of 1980, 1982 and 1988; and the Trades Union Act (1980). The unions lost powers in crucial areas: the compulsory closed shop was gradually eliminated, trade union officials were made subject to democratic elections, sympathy strikes were forbidden and industrial action could only take place after a ballot. Notice that part of Thatcher's strategy was to involve the union members themselves, not just the officials, in decisions about their industries.

She was also helped by two spectacular victories – over the print workers and the miners. The former had resisted modernization of the industry, virtually controlled recruitment to it and dictated terms to weak and craven managements. *The Times* had been out of production most of 1979 and its new owner, Rupert Murdoch, defeated union blockades by telling them that new plant was to be for a new publication when in fact it was to be used, with non-print-union workers and modern equipment, for all of News International's British publications. It was Thatcherism in practice.

Miners had defeated previous governments effortlessly and always appealed to the sentimentality that so afflicts British public life. Their leader, Arthur Scargill, embarked on a strike in 1984 ostensibly about pit closures, which split the National Union of Mineworkers. Thatcher chose her moment well and there was plenty of coal in the country when she took on Scargill in the often violent strike of 1984–85. Its defeat was a bitter blow for organized labour. Their numbers have declined from about 12 million to 8 million, they are under the law and play little part in political life.

There were areas of public policy in which whatever classical liberal predilections Thatcher might have had, were suffused by a kind of dispositional conservatism, an almost pusillanimous acceptance of things as they are, specifically welfare and health. No inroads were made into the rising welfare costs which not only were financially burdensome but also had a debilitating effect on the morale of the workforce. As she said: 'It is no part of my party's thinking to dismantle the welfare state.'[9] The family continued its long-term decline, unmarried motherhood increased and many still found welfare preferable to work. And her reluctance to use the proper market in health ensured that the country continued to be entranced by the meretricious allure of the National Health Service – 'free at the point of consumption' – despite its manifest inefficiencies.

A particularly important reform was passed in the 1986 Social Security Act which reduced some of the future costs of Barbara Castle's potentially ruinous SERPS (State Earnings Related Pension Scheme). The new law encouraged people to leave the state sector for pensions and ultimately half the population had privately funded schemes. Also the basic state pension was updated in terms of prices, not wages.

However, no real progress was made in health. The basic problem has always been that the financing and delivery of it are in the same hands – the state. In Europe it is not tax-funded but financed by social insurance with competing suppliers. At least Thatcher tried to modify the monopoly status of the NHS by separating delivery from finance, and giving doctors some independence. Health Authorities could 'buy' treatment from nominally competing Trust hospitals (which could theoretically go bankrupt) within an 'internal market'. Only if people paid for medical insurance with their own money could the patient ever achieve that independence for which she had pressed elsewhere. At the end she was reduced to uttering platitudes like 'the NHS is safe in our hands' and promises that she would make the health system so efficient that no one would want to go private. Like the dispositional conservatives, Thatcher thought that any threat to the NHS would be electoral suicide.

Thatcher was accused by her critics on the right as well as the left of 'destroying' the independence of local government with her ill-fated replacement of the rates by the Community Charge. But local government has never been independent and by the 1980s had been in the main financed by central grants. With the majority of voters being non-ratepayers there were few restraints on its profligacy. To make *all* residents pay something would have revealed the true cost of local services and might have introduced competition between local authorities. Unfortunately this was a rare occasion where her classical liberalism overcame her practical conservatism and the creation of an extra class of taxpayers proved to be politically disastrous.

Thatcher's conservatism included a coherent vision to restore Britain's status in the world. This is seen in her attitude to Europe. At one time, she was not hostile to some form of European integration, which could explain her support for the Single European Act (1986). This had good free-market credentials. Under the prevailing unanimity rule of the Council of Ministers, some Member States had persisted with anti-market policies, such as restrictions on the free movement of labour and capital and the retention of exchange controls. The introduction of qualified majority voting would end all this. However, as Thatcher soon saw, the Act simply led to a mania for harmonization and the gradual elimination of the nation state. Her Bruges speech in 1988 revealed her true feelings about Europe. It should be a loose alliance of independent states, each with its autonomous legal and political system, held together by a commitment to free trade, private property and the market. Her derisive comments about the former Commissioner, Jacques Delors, revealed that she knew instinctively what the (then) Community had become – a rent-seeker's paradise. Bureaucrats simply capture the extra economic value (rent) created by others.

Margaret Thatcher was not a theorist with a doctrine derived from first principles. Her ideas were nested in British political history from which she drew lessons rather than dogmas. Her comment, 'there is no such thing as society' tried to dispel the illusion that some strange entity could eliminate personal responsibility for action. Some individuals commit crimes and other individuals create wealth. She claimed there are only individuals and their families and it is the network of social and economic practices that they spontaneously create which constitutes society. And individuals must have freedom to so act.

What kind of ideology was Thatcherism – classical liberal or traditional conservatism with its pragmatic approach to political life? She was facing a struggle with socialism which no Conservative had faced before. Excessive public spending, manifest state inefficiency and militant trade unionism were all tearing at the fabric of society as never before. Thatcher's market theory seemed radical to some conservatives because they never had to articulate principles before. Adam Smith's ethics, as contained in *The Theory of Moral Sentiments* appealed to her. The market requires a grounding in ethics that stresses the necessity for honesty and trust in business and financial matters. We must keep our promises and respect legitimately acquired property.

In the pantheon of conservatives, Thatcherism is not very radical. The major thing that prevented the Conservative embrace of the free market was its commitment to the landed interest. It was for this reason that the Liberals became committed to small government, free trade and low taxation. It was Liberal opposition to agricultural protection (brought about by the Corn Laws) that marked their intellectual dedication to the free market. But it was the Conservatives under Robert Peel who repealed the Corn Laws. He might have split his party but it was this action (and his Tamworth Manifesto) that enabled the Conservatives to join the modern world. He could be called an ancestor of Thatcher and was a genuine modernizer, not of the ersatz variety seen amongst modern conservatives. There were some famous and revered Conservatives in the nineteenth century whom one would rarely associate with Thatcherism. Margaret Thatcher's conviction politics stands in marked contrast to Disraeli's reputed comment: 'here are my principles. If you don't like them I will change them'. Thatcher never used the Conservative slogan 'One-nation Toryism'. She would have regarded that as an appeal to the lowest common denominator and a retreat from those principles which she regarded as essential to the country's progress. If anything, Gladstone led the party of free trade, minimal government and low taxation; the very things she has always understood to be necessary convictions. His domestic policy would have had great appeal to her free-market-plus-modest-nationalist ideology. Salisbury was certainly a man of principle (witness his scathing attacks on Conservatives who had opportunistically breached with tradition over the second Reform Act of 1867) and by the time he became Prime Minister the Conservatives were no longer completely associated with the landed interest. They had become modern in outlook yet respectful of tradition and quite capable of taking up the cause of the market when Liberals more or less abandoned it after 1905. They became too associated with the burgeoning welfare state to be serious believers in individualism, freedom and small government.

Of course, there is always Winston Churchill to whom every conservative, including Margaret Thatcher, felt a duty to render some obeisance. Churchill was always a convinced anti-communist; it has also been suggested that Churchill's fear of big government, espoused in the 1945 election campaign, was inspired by Hayek's *Road to Serfdom*. Twentieth-century Conservatives could not resist the allure of the 'middle way' under Harold Macmillan and Edward Heath. The correct traditionalist conservatism had always been there but never cogently articulated until Thatcher. British conservative doctrine is rich enough to be capable of absorbing a variety of differing viewpoints. The tradition is some way from expressing unsullied classical liberalism but there is little in it that is anti-market. It was the genius of Margaret Thatcher to articulate freedom and the market and adapt principles which might seem, superficially, to be antithetical to it. At the very least, she made Conservatives think about economics and still remain conservative. Her legacy is a commitment to liberty which is not derived from the textbooks of political philosophy but from economics, history and practice. Although she did acquire some 'theory' it was usually leavened by experience and therefore more realistic than modern social science.

Notes

1   Norman Barry, *The New Right* (London: Croom Helm, 1987), Chapter 5.
2   Norman Barry, 'Burke's Political Economy', in Ian Crowe, *Edmund Burke: His Life and Legacy* (Dublin: Four Courts Press, 1997), pp. 104–14.
3   *The Anatomy of Thatcherism* (London: Fontana, 1992), Part 1.
4   If Conservatives had been more aware of that publication they would have been less likely to appropriate Burke for those moderate, market sceptics who achieved some influence over some post-War policy.
5   *Editorial Note*: The distinguished authors of the letter included Mervyn King, the present Governor of the Bank of England.
6   See Alistair B. Cooke, *In Defence of Freedom* (New York: Prometheus, 1985), p. 13. This book is a useful collection of Thatcher's speeches.
7   Ibid., p. 8. But she made clear in the same speech she did not think the majority was always right.
8   Ibid., p. 63.
9   Ibid., pp. 12–13.

12 Back from the future

William Hague

Did Margaret Thatcher put Britain on course to be Europe's biggest economy within twenty years? Former Cabinet Office and Treasury economist, Christopher Smallwood, now Barclays' Chief Economic Adviser, has predicted that Britain is apparently on course to overtake Germany as the biggest economy in Europe within a generation.[1] Economic predictions are notoriously unreliable, but if current trends in economic growth and population change continue, Britain's economy will be bigger than Germany's by the 2020s. GDP per head is already higher in Britain than in Germany, and the size of the UK economy exceeded France's at the end of the 1990s. It is undeniable that the structural changes of the 1980s initiated the sustained growth of wealth and output behind this trend. Under this scenario, reliant as it is on the extrapolation of existing trends, there can be little doubt that Margaret Thatcher's premiership will be seen as the decisive turning-point in modern British history. She accomplished changes to labour laws, pension policies, and state ownership which continental countries are still struggling to emulate. Opposition leaders have been emerging in countries such as Germany and Sweden enjoying the title of 'a new Margaret Thatcher'.

Britain's experience of anger and despair in the late 1970s may have been unique. Margaret Thatcher came to power because of the conditions in the period before the 1979 election. Growing up at that time in South Yorkshire, I witnessed in full the overbearing and incompetent state which she was determined to roll back: many of my classmates lived in council houses which their families had no opportunity to own, were expected to go on to work in nationalized industries with little option of a different career, and had been given no choice at all in which school they would attend. The general supposition was that Arthur Scargill, who lived a few miles away, was more powerful than the government of the day. We were surrounded by the evidence, as well as the statistics, of national decline: rising unemployment, a succession of strikes, and poor public services. It was, however, only the anger created by the Winter of Discontent which converted this steady sense of disillusionment into a solid Conservative majority – a majority which was only sustained through the 1980s by the convenient division of opposition forces. Would-be Thatchers in countries with proportional voting systems or less centralized national decision-making will find comparable change much harder to achieve, particularly without an eruption of public outrage similar to that of 1978–79.

The very fact that Margaret Thatcher's achievements are so widely discussed overseas illustrates her enormous impact. Her fervent insistence on what was right, her advocacy of freedom and the market economy on the basis of moral principle, aroused the wonder of people more accustomed to a technocratic approach. Recently in Japan I was taken into a garden where my hosts stood in a circle, beamed, and pointed at a piece of the ground, saying: 'Lady Thatcher, she stood here! She talked about freedom!' For it was not just in terms of ideas that Thatcher changed people's attitudes in a way that will long outlive her. She also provided a tutorial in leadership, political tactics, and the need to persist in fighting a conventional wisdom, which has changed the most basic behaviour of an entire generation of politicians. Since many of us so affected were in our teens at the time, the lessons of this tutorial will still be put into practice 25 years from now.

For one thing, her style of leadership seemed dramatically more 'presidential' than anything seen before. Her statement before taking office that 'in government, I could not waste time having internal arguments' was hugely over-optimistic, but a world away in attitude from the collegial style of Prime Ministers such as Attlee or Baldwin. She seemed to demonstrate that change in Britain could only be driven by the Prime Minister and a close-knit group in Downing Street. To those who believe that politicians are largely the prisoners of circumstances, and that the policies of Prime Ministers always reflect the majority assumptions of the time, she provided a dramatic counter-example. It was clear at the time of the Falklands War that almost none of her colleagues would have thought sending a task force to the South Atlantic a sensible idea without her emphatic insistence on it. She needed her colleagues from across the entire spectrum of Tory opinion, and the achievements of her Government in such matters as urban regeneration, council house sales, and trade union reform owed much to Ministers who did not share her overall outlook, but she always gave the Government its central driving purpose and sense of what was right. For a long time to come, she has brought strong and controlling leadership back into fashion.

In political strategy she demonstrated to aspiring politicians the power of symbolism and the potential of incrementally pursued policies. People knew that she stood for fairly dramatic change even in the initial stages of her leadership when she was more cautious about proposing it than is sometimes remembered. The initial programme of privatization and trade union reform was modest indeed and was added to over time, as the great fear that trade unions could lead the political opposition to the Government receded. On the other hand, some of her Government's initial economic moves, such as the abolition of exchange controls and switch from income tax to VAT, were instant and major breaches of political orthodoxy. She exhibited a lack of fear of confronting received wisdom or political correctness which will always be of comfort to the generations that knew her. On the night before the Hong Kong hand-over in 1997, I heard her telling a group of Latin American ambassadors: 'Well, you would not have so many problems if you had been colonized by the

British', an admonition delivered with no trace of diplomatic restraint and met only with awed silence on the part of the unfortunate ambassadors. After my own narrow by-election victory in 1989, in which water privatization proposals had cost me thousands of votes, I went to tell her that I had met no voter in favour of this policy. Many political leaders would have nodded and said they took the point; Margaret Thatcher left me in no doubt that the fault of this lay with the voters rather than the policy, an insight which was indeed borne out as the privatized industry succeeded and the controversy evaporated over subsequent years.

It is impossible to exaggerate the influence of this style on the behaviour of politicians in both main parties, and on the governing of Britain for at least a further quarter of a century. The idea that productive change came from political consensus was comprehensively shattered, and the view that popularity was always necessary received a body-blow: 'If you just set out to be liked, you would be prepared to compromise on anything at any time and you would achieve nothing.' Wise observers will have noted that this approach does have its limits. The Thatcher premiership was brought to an end by her refusal to abandon the poll tax, a policy which, ironically, was not central to what she was trying to achieve.

Tony Blair will not be the last British leader to take his cue from Margaret Thatcher as to how government should be administered, although he has a far greater need to be liked. Nor is it simply in the manner of decision-making that her successors will continue to try to emulate her. Blair's dedication to the Atlantic alliance, seemingly at any price, owes a good deal to his sense of where power lies in the world, but it also appears to be a conscious imitation of the relationship Thatcher built with Reagan. She renewed the enthusiasm and relevance of the Anglo–American bond, the importance of which is likely to become even greater over the next quarter of a century. For unless current trends go into sharp reverse, the next quarter of a century will witness the continuation of an American monopoly on the ability to project military power around the globe, and at the same time a major shrinkage in Europe's weight in world affairs. Most forecasters seem to believe that declining populations, massive pension deficits, and other major structural economic problems will see Europe slide in the coming decades from one-fifth of the world economy to one-tenth of it. By contrast, America looks set, despite its serious deficits of today, to enjoy major population growth and remain a principal driver of economic growth. It is easy to forget that many pre-Thatcher commentators saw the special relationship with America as one of declining importance and that there existed a strong consensus that Britain's place lay in a more closely integrated Europe. Margaret Thatcher was ahead of her time in steering away from this consensus and towards the distribution of power in the twenty-first century.

It follows from this that her instinctive resistance to European integration is likely to be vindicated by the events of the coming years. Attempts to ratify the EU Constitution may turn out to be the high water mark of the European 'project', and to lead to division and impasse rather than unity. That for Britain to march towards 'ever closer union' with the rest of the EU would be a great mistake is as likely to become a prevailing consensus in the next few years as was the idea that Britain had no alternative some years ago. Seen from the vantage point of a relatively fast-growing economy, it is likely to become steadily more mysterious to people as to why it was ever thought that advantage might lie in adopting more of the rules and regulations of the least dynamic part of the world economy. Every survey of British opinion shows that younger voters tend to be the least enthusiastic about such propositions as joining the euro. A major generational change in attitudes has taken place over the last 20 years which is likely to be further reinforced in the future; whereas a student of the 1980s would have gone inter-railing around Europe and perhaps had a pen-friend in France, a student of the twenty-first century spends his or her gap year in Australia and Thailand and sends emails in English all over the world. The scepticism of Thatcher about a

European future and her constant excitement about links with America and Japan are more likely to be seen by the decision-makers of the next quarter of a century as commonplace and inevitable than they ever were at the time.

As part of this worldview, Margaret Thatcher has always held to a belief in the distinctiveness of being British. The role of the 'English-speaking world' in saving democracy has always been a refrain of her private as well as public comments. Often this has been seen as old-fashioned, yet once again it is more likely to be seen as prescient by future commentators. The best hope for Britain in the world economy is to leverage its distinctive advantages of language, time zone, special links with America, the Commonwealth and Europe, and the stability that comes from having a robust democracy and judicial system. As young people from all over the world have poured into London in increasing numbers in recent years, seeking work, education and enjoyment, the distinctive appeal of Britain becomes steadily more evident. The genesis of all of this will be seen as Margaret Thatcher's premiership, and it is very much in line with her own gut attitude.

That Margaret Thatcher's premiership brought about a decisive transformation in British economic performance is a truth that is likely to become even starker as the years pass. Self-employment soared by 50 per cent during her premiership. Even the steadily rising burden of taxation and regulation under the Blair/Brown government has not yet brought to a halt the revival of enterprise and sheer sense of being able to do business which she inaugurated. Recently I appeared on 'Any Questions?' with Arthur Scargill, the very man who inspired such awe and fear in my teens. I discovered that in 2004, he was still calling for the nationalization of large parts of the economy, including super-markets, and a total respect for picket lines. What was striking was the reaction of the audience: while a pre-Thatcher audience would have trembled before him, a post-Thatcher audience simply laughs – treating his comments as a trip down memory lane, an entertaining show put on by an affable and now harmless museum piece. Such contrasts demonstrate more convincingly than any statistics the extent of the change which the Thatcher Government wrought.

Such might be the future view of Thatcher's legacy in Britain. Yet perhaps more important and far-reaching of all will be the impact of her fervour and ideas in international affairs. It would be overstating the case to argue that Margaret Thatcher set in train the revival of market economics, the wave of privatizations, and the dismantling of command economies around the world. Much of the explanation for these things lies in the operation of immense economic and social forces. Yet it would be perfectly fair to observe that Thatcher's advocacy of economic liberty as one of the fundamental guarantees of political liberty, in a way that was almost messianic, gave heart and zest to like-minded people in Eastern Europe and many other parts of the world. Today, it is indeed Conservative ideas that are advancing around the globe. From privately provided education in Sweden, Charter Schools in America, healthcare vouchers in Nicaragua, and privatized electricity in Guatemala, policies based on private provision are being adopted en masse. The importance of private ownership in achieving social stability and economic growth is now accepted in some surprising places, as demonstrated by the Czech voucher privatization scheme and the issuing of property titles to millions of urban squatters in Peru – a further radical extension of the idea of council house sales. Above all, the energizing effect of low direct tax rates is generating strong downward competitive pressure: low corporate taxes in Ireland have been an obvious success, while many Central and Eastern European countries, including Russia, are adopting a flat rate of income tax. Countries which devote a smaller than average proportion of their GDP to taxation – Australia, New Zealand, Singapore, Ireland, the USA, Japan, and Eastern European countries – will enjoy a clear competitive advantage in the coming years. With tax competition therefore set to intensify in the future, Margaret Thatcher's demolition of high tax rates in Britain will be seen as the beginning of a wave which rippled around the world.

None of this is to argue that the Thatcher legacy will be viewed as the whole and complete answer to politics, or a philosophy which can always be adhered to. Thatcherism was, in any case, an evolving mixture of attitudes rather than an abstract ideology. The Thatcher Government achieved an immense amount in eleven years, and the Major administration did much to entrench what was achieved, but it did not leave behind it the transformation of health or education services, nor produce convincing answers to crime of the kind which some American cities have more recently pioneered. Neither did it leave behind it a convincing explanation of how freer markets can proceed hand-in-hand with environmental protection, an issue likely to be ever more prominent as the years go by.

All that is clear is that the Thatcher example will always be an inspiration to those who believe in economic freedom and political order. Her view of Britain's role and opportunity in the world will be seen in the future as heralding a new and more optimistic period of our history.

Note

1   *Daily Telegraph*, 19 July 2004, reporting on a Research Paper by Christopher Smallwood, Chief Economic Adviser to Barclays Bank, July 2004.

Index

Index

Clinton, William Jefferson (Bill) 34,
  see also USA
Cockfield, Francis 40–1
Commonwealth 35, 195
communism 1, 4, 26, 31–5, 107, see
  also Marxism, Soviet Union
Conservative, Conservative Party,
  Tory Party, see also Britain,
  Economy, Labour Party,
  Liberalism, Thatcher
1922 Committee 16
amazed at election of woman leader
  16
annus mirabilis of social policy 168
appeal to traditional Labour voters 24
cadres 13
Central Office 12 (see Chapter 1)
Centre for Policy Studies 2, 19
corporatist 'Middle Way' 13
covenant between dead, living and
  unborn 103
culture of Tories 4, 12
disarray over Europe 47–4
economic determinist 179
economic liberalism not conservative
  doctrine 69
failure to understand public's support
  of marriage 85
failure to understand counter-culture
  7
family is model of relationships and
  obligations 103
Government
  1970–74 14 (see Chapter 1)
  1979–97 35 (see Chapter 2)
Hague's reforms 24 n. 1
health policy 163
helicopter 43
hierarchy 12
impression of prejudice on asylum,
  homosexuality, family 84
knights from shires 16, 22–3
leadership election of 1975 12
left of Party patrician wing 19

Listening to Britain exercise 84
Middle Way consensus under
  Macmillan and Heath 13, 178,
  188
MP image of 'middle-aged white
  married man' 84
never ideologically committed to free
  market 178
NHS 'safe with the Tories' 78
One nation Toryism 188
Research Department 13
Retreat of the State 67
Right Approach 17
sacred duty of Conservatism 103
Saxon king and noblemen analogy 12
Selsdon agenda 14
Selsdon Man 24 n. 2
Shadow Cabinet 12 (see Chapter 1)
Short Money 13
steadily more Eurosceptic 23
Tories now had a true hero 22
Tory Nationalization of Britain 67
Tory Reform Committee 13
Tory Wets 18
war on lone mothers was over 84–5
creative advances in political economy
  2, 4
Cuba, ally of Soviet Union 31
Czech privatization vouchers 196

Dark Satanic Mills 1
Delors, Jacques 4, 39, 42, 44–6, 186
Denmark 30, 48
détente 31
Disraeli, Benjamin 188
Dixon, Pauline 152
Dooge Committee 41, 48
Dooge, James 41
Duncan-Smith, Iain 85

Economy, see also Britain, Education,
  Employment, Europe, Housing,
  Liberalism, Marriage
  Anglo-Saxon market liberalization 5

Index

Index

Index

Index